365 WAYS TO
BOOST YOUR
Metabolism

**EVERYDAY TIPS
TO ACHIEVE YOUR
MAXIMUM
FAT-BURNING
POTENTIAL**

JUMPSTART
YOUR
METABOLISM,
STARTING
TODAY!

RACHEL LAFERRIERE, MS, RD

adamsmedia
Avon, Massachusetts

Copyright © 2010 by F+W Media, Inc.

Published by
Adams Media, a division of F+W Media, Inc.
57 Littlefield Street, Avon, MA 02322. U.S.A.
www.adamsmedia.com

ISBN-10: 1-4405-0580-2
ISBN-13: 978-1-4405-0580-5

Printed in the United States of America.

10 9 8 7 6 5 4 3 2 1

Library of Congress Cataloging-in-Publication Data
is available from the publisher.

This publication is designed to provide accurate and authoritative information with
regard to the subject matter covered. It is sold with the understanding that the publisher
is not engaged in rendering legal, accounting, or other professional advice. If legal advice
or other expert assistance is required, the services of a competent professional person
should be sought.

> —From a *Declaration of Principles* jointly adopted by a Committee of the
> American Bar Association and a Committee of Publishers and Associations

Many of the designations used by manufacturers and sellers to distinguish their product
are claimed as trademarks. Where those designations appear in this book and Adams
Media was aware of a trademark claim, the designations have been printed with initial
capital letters.

This book is available at quantity discounts for bulk purchases.
For information, please call 1-800-289-0963.

To Mom and Becca, for always believing in me.
We may not have it all together, but together we have it all!

Acknowledgments

I would like to thank everyone at Adams Media for their support during the creation of this book. I am forever indebted to my editor Katie Corcoran Lytle for guiding me through every step of the way. I'd also like to thank Paula Munier, Karen Cooper, Wendy Simard, Casey Ebert, Robin Witkin, Deb Baker, and Elisabeth Lariviere. And, of course, a million thanks to Shawn for cooking me dinner and cheering me on every night as I pondered and wrote.

CONTENTS

Introduction **vii**

Boost Your Metabolism by . . .

Boost Your Metabolism by . . .

INTRODUCTION

Feeling fatigued, flabby, or flustered about your health? Would you like to feel fit, fabulous, and full of energy? Well, *365 Ways to Boost Your Metabolism* is here to help! This book will teach you how to adjust your diet and lifestyle to tone your body, burn more calories, and feel fantastic about yourself.

So what is metabolism? Well, metabolism includes all of the chemical reactions in your body that occur during the conversion of food into energy. Our bodies use components of food—including carbohydrates, fat, protein, vitamins, and minerals—to produce energy and other substances necessary to sustain life. There are three major factors that make up metabolism:

- Basal metabolic rate (BMR)
- Physical activity level (PAL)
- Thermic effect of food (TEF)

Let's see how you can use these factors to make your metabolic rate skyrocket!

Basal Metabolic Rate

Basal metabolic rate measures calories burned when your body is at rest, and represents 60 to 75 percent of your total energy expenditure. Your BMR is primarily determined by your body size and body composition, but gender and age can also have an effect. Larger individuals—those who are taller or heavier—have greater metabolic rates. Those with a greater lean body mass, or fat-free mass, also have higher metabolisms. Because gender and age affect lean body mass (aging is associated with a loss of lean body mass and females have more fat in proportion to muscle than men) they also have an effect on metabolism. While you cannot change some of these factors, have no fear! The tips in this book will help you increase your fat-free mass and metabolic rate to turn your body into a calorie-burning machine.

Physical Activity Level

Physical activity, which burns a variable amount of calories depending on intensity and duration, is the only way to increase muscle mass, which, in turn, increases your BMR and total energy expenditure. From lawn mowing to tennis to lunges, you will find suggestions in the following chapters to help you become more physically fit.

The Thermic Effect of Food

Finally, the thermic effect of food measures the increase in metabolic rate caused by the digestion and absorption of nutrients following meal consumption. The amount of calories burned depends on the size of the meal, the ratio of carbohydrates to protein to fat, the amount of fiber in the meal, caffeine content, and spiciness. For example, consuming capsaicin, a molecule found in spicy foods, has been shown to boost metabolism by helping you burn more calories. The harder your body has to work to digest the foods that you eat, the higher your metabolic rate!

By adjusting any one, but preferably all three, of these factors, you will be on your way to a healthier body and lifestyle. And remember, to lose weight, calories taken in must be fewer than calories burned. After reading this book, you will not only know how to cut calories, but also how to increase the amount of calories expended by increasing your BMR, PAL, and TEF.

As a registered dietitian, I've seen countless individuals struggle with weight gain and chronic disease. But I've also seen the same individuals overcome their struggles and make amazing diet and lifestyle changes. Rest assured that, by following the recommendations in this book, you *can* meet your nutrition, fitness, and health goals.

CHAPTER 1
Boost Your Metabolism by . . .
KNOWING YOUR BODY

1. Arm Yourself with Knowledge: Metabolism Basics

Broadly defined, metabolism includes all of the physical and chemical changes that occur inside the cells of the body and that maintain life. All activity in the body occurs through the process of metabolism, in which cells break down chemicals and nutrients to generate energy and form new molecules such as proteins. Efficient metabolism requires blood loaded with oxygen, glucose, and nutrients. Enzymes are the molecules that make metabolism happen, and nutrients are the vitamins and minerals that act as essential coenzymes. When a nutrient is deficient in the body, certain metabolic functions are impeded and symptoms of disease can arise. Your metabolism is influenced by:

- Age: Metabolism naturally slows about 5 percent per decade after age thirty.
- Gender: Men generally burn more calories at rest than women.
- Muscle mass: The more lean muscle you have, the higher your metabolic rate.
- Activity level: The more you exercise, particularly aerobically, the higher your metabolic rate.
- Genes: There can be an inherited aspect; some people have sluggish metabolic rates.
- Thyroid function: You could have an overactive or underactive thyroid, but this is uncommon.

The good news: If you eat a balanced, healthy (low-fat) diet, add exercise (lots of exercise), and keep your body in top running form, your metabolism will burn calories like a top-flight engine. That's why we'll cover a wide range of topics that have to do with maximizing your overall health, nourishing your body, and exercising, all of which will help you get your body functioning at its maximum capacity and boost your metabolism!

2. Understand the Three Components

The term *metabolism* refers to the way your body processes and utilizes the food you eat, not to the amount of time required to do so. In other words, it's not how fast you metabolize food, but how efficiently you convert food into energy. The process of metabolism consists of the following three components:

1. Basal metabolism: 60 to 65 percent of the calories you eat daily provide the basic energy you need to stay alive—breathing, circulating blood, organ functioning, adjusting hormonal levels, growing and repairing cells, and so on. Even if you lie on your sofa all day, your body will burn these calories to support basic body functions. How many and how efficiently you burn calories to meet these needs is called your basal metabolic rate (BMR).
2. Physical activity: 25 percent of your calories support movement and physical activity. The frequency and intensity of physical activity can positively or negatively affect this aspect.
3. Food processing: 10 percent of calories are expended ingesting, digesting, absorbing, transporting, and storing your caloric intake. This is called the thermic effect, or the energy your body expends processing the food you eat. For example, if you eat 2,000 calories a day, approximately 10 percent, or 200 calories, will be used eating and digesting your food.

3. Understand the Two Primary Processes

Most of the food you eat is digested and then converted into energy through the process of metabolism. This process, experts say, involves a complex network of hormones and enzymes that not only convert food into fuel but also affect how efficiently you burn that fuel. Within it, there are two contrary, yet complementary, simultaneous processes:

- Catabolism. This is the breaking-down process. Your body creates energy by deconstructing digested food or stored fat into simpler substances so it can use them in other ways. Fats are broken down into glycerol and fatty acids. Carbohydrates are broken down into glucose, galactose, and fructose and used as the primary energy that fuels the body during the day. Proteins are broken down into amino acids, which the body uses to rebuild or repair tissues.
- Anabolism. This is the building-up process. Your body uses energy from glucose and other molecules to build cells, move muscles, and carry out other vital functions. For instance, the glucose from carbohydrates can be used to make glycogen chains, the glycerol and fatty acids from fats can form triglycerides, and the amino acids from proteins are used to remake other proteins.

4. Understand How Metabolism Processes Food

The way metabolism works is by causing a series of chemical reactions that break down food. How it does this depends on whether the food is a carbohydrate, protein, or fat. Without getting too clinical, it's helpful to know the basics:

1. Carbohydrates are absorbed as simple sugars, mostly glucose. When your body needs energy, it breaks down this glucose into a metabolite known as pyruvate. Depending on the amount of available oxygen, pyruvate is then converted either anaerobically (without oxygen) into lactic acid for short bursts of energy, or aerobically (with oxygen) into acetyl CoA a molecule that creates a slower, more long-term source of energy. Lactic acid may also be recycled back into glucose, but acetyl CoA cannot.

2. During the digestive process, proteins are broken down into amino acids, which are then converted into building blocks for hormones, nucleic acids (part of DNA), digestive enzymes, and antibodies. Though an amino acid's primary role is to develop and repair other proteins, it may also be used for energy and broken down into different metabolites. To be processed, amino acids are broken down further into pyruvate or into acetyl CoA, or they are moved into the citric acid cycle inside the mitochondria.

3. In the metabolic process, fats and oils are broken down into glycerol and fatty acids. Glycerol can either be built up to make glucose or broken down to form pyruvate. Like glucose, this pyruvate can then be used to form lactic acid or acetyl CoA. Fatty acids are broken down in a process known as beta, or fatty acid, oxidation, which produces acetyl CoA. During beta-oxidation, oxygen combines with fragments of the fatty acid to release electrons into the electron transport chain. Unlike glycerol, fatty acids cannot be used to create glucose.

Since all three of the main energy-producing nutrients can be broken down into acetyl CoA, they can all be used to generate fat, which the body can use as energy, or they can be stored in fat cells for future use.

5. Know the Winning Formula for Weight Maintenance

The winning formula to maintaining your weight is that as long as the amount of calories you consume equals the amount of calories you expend, your weight should remain steady. If you are taking in more calories than your body can metabolize and burn as energy and you want to lose weight, you will have to reduce the amount of calories you take in, increase the number of calories you burn through physical exercise, or most likely do both. It is difficult to lose weight without changing the output side of the metabolism equation; that is, you need to boost your metabolism and increase its efficiency by eating healthfully and by exercising regularly and rigorously.

6. Determine Your Metabolic Rate

One of the first steps to take when embarking on a health and fitness plan is to determine how many calories your body burns every day. This rate is your metabolic rate, or the rate at which your body burns calories. This number will give you a concrete idea of how many calories you need to maintain your current weight, or how many you need to cut to lose weight. Cornell University offers a Metabolic Calculator that is based on your gender, age, height, weight, and activity level. Check it out on their website *www.users.med.cornell.edu/~spon/picu/calc/beecalc.htm.*

7. Understand Why Your Metabolic Rate Drops with Weight Loss

Surprisingly, the more weight you carry, the faster your metabolism. Having to carry around the extra weight forces your metabolism to fire up. Sounds good, but this creates that infamous weight-loss wall. As you lose weight, your body doesn't need to work as hard to metabolize food into energy, so it slows down the process. This accounts for the day every dieter experiences when the needle on the scale seems stuck and unlikely ever to move southward again. Unfortunately, the only way to combat this plateau is to stick with the diet and increase the amount and/or intensity of your workouts. The slimmer you become, the fewer calories you'll need to maintain good health—deal with it.

8. Understand Why Metabolism Slows with Age

Around age thirty, the immune system fights a little slower; the muscular system loses tone; the ratio of muscle to fat declines; fat settles around the stomach, buttocks, and thighs; the abdomen sags—and the metabolism begins to change. With age-related decrease in muscle mass comes a decline in metabolism and a decrease in calories burned. You will gain weight more easily and find it more difficult to lose, and your digestive tract, which used to be able to handle anything you popped into it, becomes sluggish and decidedly more sensitive. At the same time, a decrease in glucose tolerance increases the risk of developing diabetes (especially if you're overweight), and increased blood pressure puts you at greater risk of heart disease (especially if you add a lot of salt to your food). As you pass your fortieth birthday, the heart muscle may enlarge so it can pump more blood as it tries to compensate for clogged and hardening arteries. At the same time, the covering sheath around the heart may thicken, resulting in an overall reduction in blood output. This decrease leads to a decline in the supply of oxygen to muscle tissue, resulting in a reduction in aerobic capacity. Bottom line: Even minimal exercise hits you harder and tires you more quickly, which slows your metabolism. To boost your metabolism despite your age, stay active—even if it becomes harder to do so.

9. Know Why Men Burn More Calories than Women

Males generally have a 10 to 15 percent faster BMR than females because the male body has a larger percentage of lean muscle tissue. The simple fact is that muscle burns calories faster than fat. The more muscle you have, the more calories you burn, even at rest.

10. Know Your Cholesterol Numbers

When you embark on any health or fitness regime, it is important to ask your doctor for a total lipoprotein profile so that you are aware not only of your total cholesterol but of each component as well. You may have a total cholesterol level that is desirable, but that doesn't mean your HDL (high-density lipoprotein or "good" cholesterol) and LDL (low-density lipoprotein or "bad" cholesterol) levels are in line. Cholesterol levels are measured by measured by milligrams per deciliter or mg/dL, which basically tells you how much cholesterol (in mg) is present in each deciliter (dL) of blood sample. Your total cholesterol level will fall into one of three categories:

1. Desirable: less than 200 mg/dL
2. Borderline high risk: 200–239 mg/dL
3. High risk: 240 mg/dL and over

If you fall within the high-risk range, you have at least twice the risk of heart disease as someone in the desirable range.

If you have a cholesterol reading over 240 mg/dL or you have risk factors such as heart disease along with cholesterol readings over 200 mg/dL, your doctor will probably prescribe a cholesterol-lowering medication in combination with a healthy low-fat diet and exercise. Diet and exercise are two important ways to both cut your cholesterol numbers and enhance your metabolism. Your doctor should periodically test your blood cholesterol levels to check on your progress.

If your numbers are high, take measures to lower them, using this as motivation to improve your nutrition, ramp up your exercise, increase your metabolism, and lose weight.

11. Know If Your Liver Is Healthy

Your liver is responsible for burning most of the fat in your body. If it is healthy, it pumps out excess fat through bile and helps you keep a healthy weight. However, if your liver is not healthy, it can cause your body to hold on to fat and cause other health problems. You can damage your liver by drinking too much alcohol, taking antibiotics or painkillers for long periods, taking oral synthetic hormone replacement drugs, being exposed to toxic chemicals including pesticides, having a viral infection of the liver (such as hepatitis C and B, autoimmune hepatitis, hemochromatosis, or primary biliary cirrhosis), or eating an unhealthful diet high in fat.

If you suspect liver problems, or if you are obese, ask your doctor to perform blood tests that will measure liver enzymes. Elevated enzymes may indicate inflammation and damage to the liver cells and their membranes. Luckily, liver cells are very resilient, and you can restore their health by following your doctor's recommendations, which may include changing your eating habits so you're on a proper diet.

12. Know Your Body Rhythms

Are you a morning person or an evening person? If you are one extreme or the other, you already know your body's preferred rhythm, and I hope you're in sync with it. If you aren't sure, or if it varies widely, pay attention to your body for a week, noticing when you are energized and when you are winding down. If your energy peaks midday, eat your highest calorie meal for lunch, or breakfast, and work out closest to the energy peak. Eating or exercising when your body is energized will maximize the metabolic burn.

13. Talk to Your Doctor If You Suspect Thyroid Problems

Thyroid hormones stimulate many metabolic activities in most body tissues, resulting in an increase in basal metabolic rate. Though it is uncommon, carrying excess (or not enough) weight may be the result of an overactive or underactive thyroid gland. Your doctor will be able to check your symptoms and run the necessary blood tests to determine if it is the cause for your battle with your weight. Some symptoms of a thyroid problem include:

- Feeling nervous, weak, or fatigued
- Having hands that shake, a heart that beats fast when at rest, and breathing problems

- Having sweaty or warm, red, itchy skin
- Experiencing more bowel movements than usual
- Having fine, soft hair that falls out
- Losing weight even though you haven't changed or have increased your diet

14. Talk to Your Doctor If You Are Diabetic

Other hormones, specifically insulin and glucagon, play an important role in metabolism by affecting glucose levels or the transport of glucose through the body. The more insulin you produce—or take—the more sluggish your metabolism will be. If you are diabetic, you must consult your doctor before embarking on any diet or exercise plan.

15. Talk to Your Doctor If You Are Pregnant or Breastfeeding

Pregnancy and breastfeeding will affect your metabolic rate. To support the growth of a fetus, a pregnant woman must take in more calories. Breastfeeding an infant also requires additional caloric intake. Both of these actions increase your rate of metabolism. Since these are very important physical events that require increased attention to nutrition and monitoring, please consult your doctor and ask for his or her input on what and how much you should be eating while pregnant or nursing.

CHAPTER 2
Boost Your Metabolism by . . .
BEING KNOWLEDGEABLE ABOUT NUTRITION

16. Understand Why Good Nutrition Is So Important

Nutrition—the science of food and its effect on our bodies—is relatively new, at least in comparison to other sciences. But at this point, the science has singled out about forty specific nutrients, each of which fulfills one of three functions in the body: gives energy, helps grow and repair tissue, or regulates metabolism. Nutrients include water, vitamins, and minerals (which grow and repair tissue) and carbohydrates, fat, and protein (which give energy by providing calories). All of the nutrients regulate your metabolism by helping your body function smoothly and in balance. Nutrition is about fueling the body for optimum function, so this chapter will provide basic suggestions for providing the nutrients you need to achieve maximum metabolism.

17. Make Nutrition a Priority

Nutrition, perhaps more than any other factor, plays an essential role in our overall health, how efficiently we metabolize our food, and how long we live. The foods we eat affect every cell, organ, and system within our bodies, so it is important to make good choices. According to nutrition experts, a healthy diet provides our body with everything it needs to operate efficiently to repair damage, for cells to reproduce, and for us to flush out toxins. Healthful foods provide us with fuel that burns for a long time and helps us have a healthy immune system. Healthful foods also give our bodies the right kind of fuel so that we have plenty of energy and a strong immune system, and they can help lower the risk of heart disease, cancer, and osteoporosis as we age.

18. Follow American Heart Association Guidelines

The American Heart Association's dietary guidelines provide useful parameters for optimum health—and optimum health leads directly to optimum metabolism.

- Dietary fat intake should be between 25 and 35 percent of total calories.
- Saturated fat intake should be less than 7 percent of total calories.
- Polyunsaturated fat should not exceed 10 percent of total calories.
- Cholesterol intake should not exceed 300 milligrams per day.
- Carbohydrate intake should represent 45 to 65 percent of total calories with emphasis on complex carbohydrates.
- Protein intake should constitute the remainder of the calories.
- Sodium intake should be limited to fewer than 2300 milligrams per day.
- Alcohol consumption is not recommended, but if consumed, it should not exceed one to two drinks per day for men and one drink per day for women. One drink is 1 to 1.5 ounces a day of hard liquor, 4 ounces of wine, or 12 ounces of beer.

19. Make Healthful Food Choices

Here's reality: Some foods are very good for your body (and your metabolism); some are not. We'll go over choices in greater detail in coming chapters, but here are the basics:

1. Eat foods that improve your health, such as:
   - Omega-3 fatty acids found in fish, flax oil, and spinach
   - Colorful vegetables that are rich in antioxidants
   - Whole foods such as brown rice, whole wheat bread and pasta, and legumes
   - Lean protein from organic meats, fish, soy, and legumes

2. Limit foods that have an adverse effect on your health, such as:
   - Excess saturated fat (meat, cheese, and fried food)
   - Trans fats (margarines, baked goods, chips, and fast food)
   - High-calorie food
   - Refined carbohydrates like white rice, white bread, chips, pasta, and cookies

20. Understand How Your Caloric Intake Affects Your Metabolism

Calories provide energy for your body, but your metabolism decides how it's going to use the calories you eat. If you take in more calories than your body requires, your body will generally store the extra calories as fat. Therefore, when you consume more calories than you need over a period of time, you gain weight. If you take in fewer calories than your body requires, or burn calories via exercise, your body will call upon the stores of fat to meet its energy requirements. If you do this over a period of time, you will lose weight.

21. Choose Your Calories Carefully

Empty-calorie foods are foods that often have a high number of calories, but few to no nutrients. These foods can pack on the pounds and give you energy, but they don't help your body become and remain healthy.

As an example: You burn about 40 calories an hour watching TV. A bowl of ice cream is about 400 calories. If you eat ice cream while watching TV, you are taking in 400 calories and burning 40 calories an hour; that is, you're taking in more calories than you're burning. And—most ice cream calories aren't nutritious. Yes, there's calcium, but other than that, there is a high amount of fat and very little fiber, vitamins, minerals, or antioxidants. If you were striving to eat a nutrient-dense diet and still wanted to eat 400 calories, you could have, for instance, a tomato (40 calories) and carrots (30 calories), sprouts (25 calories), grilled chicken (200 calories), and a glass of red wine (90 calories). And if you wanted to splurge and still get a hit of something rich and decadent (like the ice cream), you could have 2 ounces of dark chocolate. Obviously this second choice would provide calories packed with nutrients, calories that nourished your body and boosted your metabolism!

22. Understand Macronutrients

Nutrients are grouped into six different categories: carbohydrates, proteins, fats, vitamins, minerals, and water. Carbohydrates, proteins, and fats are called macronutrients because we need larger amounts of them in our diet. Some foods consist of one, two, or all three of these macronutrients. Even though each macronutrient has a particular function in the body, they work in partnership for good health. Our bodies need all three macronutrients to function properly, but we don't need them in equal amounts. Some evidence suggests that a diet with macronutrients in the wrong proportions is a risk factor for diseases like coronary heart disease and certain cancers. Achieving the right balance, quantity, and quality of macronutrients will keep your body healthy and your metabolism functioning at its peak capacity.

23. Understand Micronutrients

A healthy diet consists not only of optimal portions of macronutrients (food) but also recommended levels of essential micronutrients. Micronutrients include vitamins and minerals. Vitamins are called "micro" nutrients because they are needed only in small amounts to do their jobs properly. Don't let the "micro" fool you, though; good things come in small packages! The micronutrients are just as essential as the macronutrients in helping to keep your metabolism functioning at a high level.

24. Understand Simple Carbohydrates

Carbohydrates, sometimes called carbs, fuel our brain and muscles and supply us with quick energy. Each gram contains 4 calories, and there are two types of carbohydrates: simple and complex. Simple carbohydrates are sugars—including glucose, sucrose, lactose, galactose, maltose, and fructose—and are found in refined sugar, fruits, milk, and yogurt. Most of your simple carbohydrate choices should come from fruits and dairy products, which also contain vitamins, minerals, and fiber and are guaranteed to help your metabolism soar!

25. Understand Complex Carbohydrates

Complex carbohydrates are long chains of molecules that are chemically more complex than simple carbohydrates. They are also considered to be more healthful because they are digested more slowly than simple carbohydrates, provide the body with a deeper pool of energy, and may include fiber. Look for high-fiber complex carbohydrates in such foods as beans, nuts, vegetables, and whole grains.

26. Eat More Complex Carbohydrates

If you crave carbohydrates, you should reach for a complex carbohydrate instead of a simple one. This is because complex carbs take longer to break down into absorbable sugars. In addition, some complex carbohydrates have the benefit of being high in fiber which helps you stay full longer, and they are usually low in calories and fat. After being processed, complex carbohydrates are stored in the liver and muscles as glycogen until they are needed. Good sources of complex carbs include nuts, vegetables, beans, whole grains, and whole-wheat or brown rice pasta. Stay away from unhealthier versions like white pasta and white bread.

27. Get Those Radicals under Control

A free radical is an unstable molecule that is formed when molecules within the body's cells react with oxygen. It is unstable because it has an unpaired electron that steals a stabilizing electron from another molecule, potentially causing cell and DNA damage. Free radicals age your body—and slow your metabolism. In fact, your metabolic process causes free radicals, but there are also external sources such as pollution.

Antioxidants are vitamins and minerals such as magnesium, selenium, vitamin C, and vitamin E that neutralize free radicals. If there aren't enough antioxidants available, excess free radicals begin to damage and destroy normal healthy cells, leading to degenerative diseases and a slow metabolism. Free radicals can damage any body structure by affecting proteins, enzymes, fats, and even DNA. They are implicated in more than sixty different health conditions, including Alzheimer's disease, heart disease, autoimmune diseases, and cancer. Vitamins C and E are natural antioxidants that may clean up roving free radicals before they can inflict damage; obtaining them from eating a varied, balanced, healthy diet is crucial.

28. Be Pro-Antioxidants

With aging, the body's stores of antioxidants diminish unless they are regularly replenished with an excellent diet or supplements. When free radicals build up in all parts of the body, they can enter nerve cells, disrupt function, and cause cell death. They can also trigger a cascade of free radical formation. This chain reaction can cause widespread oxidative damage in the brain and body. To maintain optimum health and boost your metabolism, include plenty of antioxidants in your diet. Foods particularly high in antioxidants include:

- Berries: wild blueberries, cranberries, blackberries, raspberries, strawberries
- Apples: Red Delicious, Granny Smith, Gala

- Beans: small red beans, red kidney beans, pinto beans, dried black beans
- Other fruits: dried prunes, sweet cherries, black plums, plums
- Other foods: artichokes, almonds, russet potatoes, tea

29. Know the Facts about Sugar

The typical American diet is packed with sugar, and most nutrition experts agree that Americans need to cut back. There is no current Recommended Dietary Allowance (RDA) for sugar, but experts recommend that about 45 to 65 percent of total calories in your diet should come from carbohydrates, with less than 10 percent coming from simple sugars. The USDA advises people who eat a 2,000-calorie healthful diet to try to limit themselves to about 10 teaspoons (40 grams) of added sugars per day. Consuming more sugar, if it pushes you over your daily calorie requirement, may lead to weight gain and a more sluggish metabolism.

30. Limit Simple Sugars

Sugars are simple carbohydrates that the body uses as a source of energy. During digestion, all carbohydrates break down into sugar, or blood glucose. Some sugars occur naturally, such as in dairy products (as lactose) and fruits (as fructose). Other foods have added sugars, or sugar that is added in processing or preparation. Most foods containing added sugars provide calories but little in the way of essential nutrients such as fiber, vitamins, and minerals. It is much healthier to consume sugars that are found naturally in foods, as these foods likely contain metabolism-revving vitamins and minerals (like calcium from milk or vitamin C from an orange). Sugar can be part of a healthy diet if consumed in moderation.

31. Always Look for Secret Sugar

There are many ways to disguise the word *sugar* on a food label. Here's a big list of what doesn't sound like sugar, but definitely is sugar: high-fructose corn syrup, fruit juice concentrate, sucrose, glucose, dextrose, honey, molasses, brown sugar, corn sweetener, corn syrup, fructose, and invert sugar. You'll find these sugars on many food labels—and if it's in the top four ingredients, there's a lot of it.

32. Avoid High-Fructose Corn Syrup

Although you may have seen ads telling you there's nothing wrong with high-fructose corn syrup, there is. This ingredient, which is found in many processed foods, is essentially pure sugar. And, when you eat it, your body releases excess insulin, which then decreases your metabolism. It also may reduce the body's ability to process the appetite-suppressing protein leptin found in healthy foods like fish. Also, fructose is more readily metabolized to fat in the liver than glucose. To keep your metabolism burning at an optimal rate, try not to eat more than 40 grams of added sugar per day, which does not include sugars found in fruit.

33. Avoid Sugar-Free Substances

A recent study published in *Behavioral Neuroscience* reports that use of artificial sweeteners may make it difficult to control calorie intake and weight. Our bodies usually rev up metabolism in preparation for a meal. In this study, however, compared to rats exposed to glucose, rats exposed to saccharin had a smaller increase in core temperature (metabolic boost) after eating a high-calorie meal. Moreover, authors hypothesize that artificial sweeteners may disrupt the body's natural ability to use sweetness as a measure of caloric content. This may trick the body into thinking sugary foods are low in calories, leading you to overeat. In order to boost your metabolism—and make it count—try eating foods that have natural sugars like apples, pears, and apricots.

34. Eat Organic Foods

Because organic foods are not subjected to pesticides, they retain more of their natural nutrients and fewer free radicals. This helps maintain cellular health, which in turn helps your body burn foods more efficiently, effectively boosting your metabolism. If you have to economize, opt for organic fruits and vegetables whose skin you eat (apples, pears, peaches, grapes, cherries, peppers, cucumbers, tomatoes, potatoes, green beans), as well as meat, eggs, and milk. Farmers' markets are great resources for organic foods, but you can also look in the phone book or online to find local farms or distributors of organic foods.

35. Maintain a Balanced Diet

You know it's important to eat healthfully. Making poor food choices or eating poor combinations of foods can result in your body producing too much or too little insulin, which can cause fatigue, irritability, weight gain, low blood sugar, and eventually, even Type 2 diabetes. There are three sources we derive energy from: carbohydrates, proteins, and fats.

Most North Americans get close to 60 percent of their calories from carbohydrates, most of which are simple carbohydrates that break down too rapidly and cause the pancreas to overload the blood with insulin. This leads to the body storing excess fat. Instead, dine on high-fiber complex carbohydrates that require the body to work harder to break down and don't overload your system with sugar.

Protein is essentially the anti-carbohydrate. The digestion of protein stimulates the release of glucagon, which causes the body to release stored carbohydrates in the liver and give the brain blood sugar, which decreases fogginess and irritability.

The final key components to a healthy diet are essential fats. They slow down the entry of carbohydrates into the bloodstream and help you to feel full.

You should aim to receive 45 to 65 percent of your calories from healthy carbohydrates, 10 to 35 percent from lean protein, and 25 to 35 percent from essential fats. To achieve this type of hormonally balanced meal, include selections from the following three sections:

- Energy-dense carbohydrates: whole grains, beans, vegetables, and fruits that contain fiber
- High-quality protein: fish, poultry, lean meats, soy, tofu, and low-fat dairy products
- Essential fats in small quantities: olive oil, avocados, and nuts

36. Learn to Eyeball Portions

To follow a healthy diet, you don't need to weigh and measure all of your food each day. Just keep in mind that portion sizes are meant as general guidelines; the aim is to come close to the recommended serving sizes, on average, over several days. Use these visual comparisons to help estimate your portion sizes:

- A 3-ounce portion of cooked meat, poultry, or fish is about the size of a deck of playing cards.
- A medium potato is about the size of a computer mouse.
- A cup of rice or pasta is about the size of a fist or a tennis ball.
- A cup of fruit or a medium apple or orange is the size of a baseball.
- A half-cup of chopped vegetables is about the size of three regular ice cubes.
- A 3-ounce portion of grilled fish is the size of your checkbook.
- An ounce piece of cheese is the size of four dice.
- A teaspoon of peanut butter equals one die; 2 tablespoons is about the size of a golf ball.
- An ounce of snack foods—pretzels, etc.—equals a large handful.
- A thumb tip equals 1 teaspoon; 3 thumb tips equal 1 tablespoon; and a whole thumb equals 1 ounce.

37. Check the Serving Size on Labels

Don't forget to check serving sizes when you read nutritional labels. This can wreak havoc on your waistline, particularly when it comes to carbohydrate and fat consumption—and we know that overeating is a big metabolism buster. For instance, a small bag of chips may read 120 calories per serving. Pay close attention and you'll know if that small bag is packing two servings and 240 calories. A regular-size bag of chips, even veggie chips, can run close to 1,000 calories—if you eat half the bag, you're consuming mega-calories.

CHAPTER 3
Boost Your Metabolism by . . .
SPICING UP YOUR LIFE

38. Set It on Fire

Capsaicin—a molecule found in spicy foods such as peppers, certain spices, Tabasco sauce, and salsa—has been shown to decrease cholesterol absorption and increase enzymes that help metabolize fat. Cayenne or ground red pepper contains the most capsaicin, but all red peppers, including milder forms of chili powder and paprika, have been found to increase calorie burning and are surprisingly good sources of antioxidants. However, it works like this: the hotter the pepper the greater the capsaicin. To punch up these positive effects, particularly to increase a feeling of satiety, pair the spicy sauces with protein. Some studies suggest that capsaicin can help boost your metabolism by as much as 50 percent for three hours after ingestion.

39. Eat Red and Green Chili Peppers

One of the most popular ways to boost your metabolism is by dining on green and red chilies. Studies have shown that people tend to eat less food when they are flavored with these antioxidant-rich peppers, which also have a positive impact on your body's cholesterol levels.

40. Add Cayenne

Cayenne not only boosts your metabolism, it serves as a potent stimulant for the whole body and a tonic for the nervous system. Recently, research has suggested that cayenne can also ease the severe pain of shingles and migraines. So spice up your meals and feel good about it. Luckily for us all, cayenne is readily available in powdered form or as a bottled hot sauce.

41. Curry Favor

Next time you're out at the grocery store or an Indian restaurant, order some curry. One of the primary ingredients in curry, turmeric, aids digestion by stimulating the flow of bile and the breakdown of dietary fats. It is a powerful source of antioxidants, containing within a single teaspoon as many antioxidants as in a half cup of grapes. Its antioxidant and anti-inflammatory capabilities can be traced back to curcumin, which gives turmeric its characteristic yellow color. For centuries, curcumin alone has been used to cure everything from heartburn to arthritis and, according to Earl Mindell's *Herb Bible*, "the herbs that are combined to make curry help prevent heart disease and stroke by reducing cholesterol and preventing clots."

42. Grab Some Ginger

Ginger has been shown to increase thermogenesis—a fancy way to say it fires up your body's furnace—which equals a boost in your body's ability to metabolize food. An Australian study found that ginger may increase metabolic rates by as much as 20 percent for a short time after it is eaten. Ginger may also lower cholesterol and has as many antioxidants as a cup of spinach. Be careful, however. If ginger is used with anticoagulants it may increase the risk of bleeding and may increase risk of hypoglycemia when used with insulin.

43. Try Cumin Seeds

Cumin seeds stimulate the metabolism by turning up the body's internal heat, but they are also rich in iron and may help promote the secretion of pancreatic enzymes, which aid in digestion and the absorption of nutrients. Cumin has also been thought to be able to improve the functioning of our immune systems and help the liver process the body's toxins. In fact, recent studies have indicated that this powerful little seed may reduce the risk of stomach and liver tumors in animals. However, patients with bile duct obstruction, gallstones, and GI disorders (including stomach ulcers and hyperacidity disorders) should avoid using cumin.

44. Harness Some Horseradish

Horseradish, a popular ingredient to add to spicy foods and mustard, helps boost metabolism by stimulating digestion, especially of fatty foods. Studies have also shown that it may increase the liver's ability to process toxins and suppress the growth of cancer cells because of the glucosinolates that it contains. These compounds can also be found in lower levels within cruciferous vegetables like broccoli and Brussels sprouts.

45. Surrender the Salt; Go Heavy on the Black Pepper

While salt has deleterious effects on your health, studies suggest black pepper may boost your metabolism in addition to helping dissolve fats and relieve symptoms caused by heartburn and indigestion. The active chemical in black pepper (piperine) triggers parts of the brain and the nervous system, which, in turn, boosts your metabolism and burns calories. So, skip the salt and instead pepper your food lavishly.

46. Bring on the Mustard

England's Oxford Polytechnic Institute discovered that eating a tea-spoon of hot mustard—not the mellow yellow, but the spicy browns—with your meal will boost metabolism 20 to 25 percent for several hours after eating.

47. Sprinkle on the Cinnamon

Researchers at the U.S. Agricultural Research Service have theorized that a substance called MHCP—found in cinnamon—may help fat cells become more responsive to the insulin needed to increase glucose (sugar) metabolism. Instead of butter, try sprinkling cinnamon on your whole-grain bread or oatmeal to save fat calories and boost your metabolism. You can also sprinkle cinnamon in your coffee, tea, or yogurt.

48. Eat Thai Food

Thai food often contains many of the spices mentioned earlier—tur-meric, cumin, black pepper, horseradish, and even cinnamon—as well as coriander and nutmeg. All these ingredients contain the magical fat-burning molecule capsaicin that will boost your metabolism by firing up your furnace and increasing metabolic activity.

49. Make Your Own Spice Splash

Now that you know the virtues and benefits of spices, create your own super-charged, metabolism-burning combinations and find ways to add a lot of spice to your life. Here are some ideas from spice specialists, McCormick:

- Sprinkle store-bought or homemade hummus or guacamole with paprika. Or, add a kick by stirring in ¼ teaspoon ground red pepper or crushed red pepper.
- Serve bread with olive oil as it's done in an Italian restaurant. Mix ¼ cup olive oil, 1 teaspoon grated Parmesan cheese, ½ teaspoon garlic powder, ⅛ teaspoon crushed red pepper, and sea salt to taste in small shallow dish.

CHAPTER 4

Boost Your Metabolism by . . .

EATING PLENTY OF LEAN PROTEIN

50. Understand the Importance of Proteins

Proteins, which are made up of amino acids, work within the body as primary building blocks for all tissues and cells, including your muscles. Their secondary function is to provide energy after your carbohydrate resources have been depleted—boosting your metabolism! One gram of protein equals 4 calories and it can be found in meat, fish, eggs, dairy, and legumes (beans and peas). While legumes are low in fat and high in fiber, animal sources of protein (which can be higher in unwanted fats) can deliver all of the necessary amino acids, so it's important to have a balance of the two to lose weight effectively.

Basically, to help your body to function properly, you must feed it protein. There are many different types of proteins—some healthy, some not so healthy—and this chapter contains many different healthy options that are better than yet another hamburger.

51. Eat More Lean Protein

Your body has to work twice as hard to digest protein as carbohydrates or fats, which means your metabolism has to work harder, too. Also, a study published in the *American Journal of Clinical Nutrition* found that when people ate more protein and cut down on fat, they reduced their calorie intake by 441 calories a day. In fact, experts think that eating protein actually enhances the effect of leptin, a hormone that helps the body feel full. When you choose protein, reach for the healthier choices, such as fish, skinless chicken, lean pork, tofu, nuts, beans, eggs, and low-fat dairy products, with the occasional lean red meat.

52. Eat Less Red Meat

Red meat contains more fat and calories than lean chicken, pork, or fish. Cutting back on red meat may help lower your risk of serious illness later in life, including heart disease, stroke, diabetes, and certain forms of cancer. It will also help lower your caloric intake, thus boosting your metabolism. When you do eat red meat, make sure it's lean and well cooked. If you hate the idea of surrendering red meat, at least cut back to red meat twice a week maximum.

53. Eat More Fish

Fish and shellfish are excellent sources of protein that are also low in fat. One serving (3 ounces) of most fish and shellfish provides about 20 grams of protein, which is approximately one third of the recommended daily amount for the average adult. In addition, fish contain all of the essential amino acid our bodies need to function and have other important minerals like iron, zinc, and, in those fish with edible bones, calcium.

As you may know, fish are also rich in omega-3 fatty acids, which promote the development of healthy membranes that make it easier for your body to use stored fat and sugar for energy. Even better, those who dine often on fish may have more leptin in their system, a hormone linked with high metabolism, appetite control, and weight loss.

The American Heart Association recommends that you eat fish rich in omega-3 fatty acids (mackerel, lake trout, herring, sardines, albacore tuna, and salmon) at least twice a week in order to reap all of its benefits.

54. Eat an Egg

Once the victim of a bad rap, nutritional research has shown that an egg has protein (in the white part) and fat (in the yellow part), but no carbohydrates. The egg white has few other nutrients, while the yellow has a high amount of vitamin B12 and folate. Nutritionists used to think that eggs contained too much fat, but they now know that the fat in an egg doesn't contribute to higher levels of cholesterol in the blood.

However, one large egg contains does 213 mg cholesterol in its yolk, and the American Heart Association recommends consuming not more than 300 mg cholesterol daily. Also, people with high cholesterol levels should eat less than 200 mg of cholesterol per day. Only eat eggs if you can fit them within the 300 mg/day limit and be especially careful if you have high LDL cholesterol or are taking a blood cholesterol–lowering medication.

55. Bolster Your Amino Acids

Amino acids, simply put, are organic compounds that make up proteins and are essential to human metabolism. Though they don't receive nearly as much mention in nutrition discussions as vitamins and minerals, amino acids are just as necessary to our health. Let's take a closer look at some of the most important amino acids in terms of boosting your metabolism—and protecting your brain:

- **Arginine**: This amino acid is partially converted into a chemical known as spermine, which is believed to help the brain process memory. Low levels of spermine often signal age-related memory loss. Arginine has also shown importance in immune function.

- **Choline:** The brain uses this amino acid to manufacture a memory-related neurotransmitter called acetylcholine. Older people are encouraged to take choline supplements (no more than 3.5 grams per day) because we tend to produce less acetylcholine as we age, putting us at greater risk of memory impairment. Choline is also important for the transport and metabolism of cholesterol. Dietary sources of choline include cabbage, cauliflower, eggs, peanuts, and lecithin.

- **Glutamine:** This amino acid is a precursor of a calming neurotransmitter known as GABA. It helps improve clarity of thought and boosts alertness by assisting in the manufacture of glutamic acid, a compound known for its ability to eliminate metabolic wastes in the brain. Glutamine is also a necessary fuel for intestinal cells.

- **Methionine:** Like glutamine, this amino acid helps cleanse the brain of damaging metabolic wastes. It is an effective antioxidant and helps reduce brain levels of dangerous heavy metals such as mercury.

56. Try Tyrosine

Tyrosine is one of the 20 amino acids that are used by cells to synthesize proteins, but studies have also shown that it may reduce stress, improve memory, and lower blood pressure even when the subject is feeling tense, all of which aids in generating a healthy metabolism. It is a building block for several neurotransmitters that affect mood. Additionally, some scientists have found that tyrosine may affect thyroid hormone levels in such a way that boosts metabolism. To get more tyrosine in your diet, dine on foods such as turkey, fish, chicken, nuts, and dairy products. If you choose to take a supplement, ingest it a half hour before meals and with a multivitamin-mineral complex that will help break it down into the chemicals you need. Be careful though. Tyrosine may cause a severe blood pressure increase in people taking the antidepressant medications known as MAOIs. It may also raise thyroid levels when taken with synthetic thyroid hormones. No one should take tyrosine at the same time as levodopa, a Parkinson's drug. Be sure to consult your physician before starting, or radically changing, any physical, nutritional, or supplemental regimen.

57. Learn about Alternate Sources of Protein

Meat, fish, and fowl may be the most obvious sources of protein, but there are plenty of plants that can provide more than enough of this powerful nutrient. Soybeans (used to make tofu), beans, nuts, peanut butter, sunflower seeds, and pumpkin seeds are awesome choices. Protein is a vital component of a healthy body, so be sure to include high-octane protein in your diet.

58. Become a Vegetarian

Vegetarians tend to be leaner than the rest of us because they don't eat fattening meat products, or at least opt mostly for less fattening sources of protein. Vegetarians don't eat meat, poultry, or fish, and a small percentage of strict vegetarians avoid animal products altogether. Others may consume eggs and/or dairy products. You don't have to go extremist right off the bat, but you may want to consider the metabolism boost you could get by adopting some habits of vegetarians or eating like a vegetarian a few days a week. Vegetarians can be classified into several different categories:

- **Vegan or strict vegetarian**: Consumes absolutely no animal foods, including foods with animal product as ingredients (These are the strictest types of vegetarians.)
- **Lacto-vegetarian**: Consumes dairy foods but no other animal foods including eggs
- **Lacto-ovo-vegetarian**: Consumes dairy foods plus eggs, but no other animal foods
- **Semi-vegetarian**: Follows a mostly vegetarian diet (lacto-ovo-vegetarian), but consumes meat, poultry, and fish occasionally

Note: Vegetarian diets can cause nutritional imbalances if they are not planned correctly. A healthy, well-planned vegetarian diet contains lots of fiber and is low in fat, especially saturated fat, and cholesterol. It also tends to be low in calories and high in certain vitamins and minerals. Read up on vegetarian diets and talk to your doctor before making a huge shift in your eating habits.

59. Try Tofu

Tofu is made from crushing soybeans and turning them into a curd that serves as a marvelous source of protein. Unlike foods from animal sources, soy is cholesterol-free. It contains no saturated fat, is a great source of fiber, contains calcium, vitamin E, and B vitamins, and is rich in the two polyunsaturated fats essential to optimal health. Soy foods may also aid in diabetes control by slowing the absorption of glucose (blood sugar) into the bloodstream and keeping blood sugar levels steadier. Most soy foods are also high in iron and are an excellent source of protein compared to other plant sources. Substitute tofu in recipes and reap all the benefits—plus take delight in knowing that it will boost your metabolism.

60. Chew on Sunflower Seeds

Sunflower seeds are a low-calorie option for protein that also happen to be a good source of magnesium, copper, selenium, phosphorous, folate, manganese, B5, vitamin E, and phytosterols. Vitamin E is the body's primary fat-soluble antioxidant that stops free radicals from damaging cell membranes and brain cells. The vitamin has also been shown to reduce the risk of colon cancer and hot flashes in menopausal women. Sunflower seeds also contain phytosterols—cholesterol-like compounds that are found only in plants and can actually reduce your own cholesterol levels, pump up your immune system, and help prevent cancer. So toss some seeds on your salads or breakfast cereals, or munch on a handful as a snack for a healthy metabolic boost.

61. Fall in Love with Beans

Beans are so jam-packed with nutrients that they qualify as both a vegetable and a protein. That's kind of like being both king and queen! Cynthia Sass, RD, considers beans a miracle food. "If I could eat only one food for the rest of my life, it would definitely be beans . . . (they) have such an amazing nutrition track record. Bean eaters are associated with smaller waist sizes and a 22-percent lower risk of obesity. They also take in less 'bad' fat and one-third more fiber than those who avoid these nutritional gems."

According to Sass, a cup of beans provides a whopping 13 grams of fiber (half of our daily requirement), about 15 grams of protein, and dozens of key nutrients, including calcium, potassium, and magnesium. Eating 3 cups of beans every week is recommended. Here are Sass's suggestions:

- **Buy canned**: Though bagged beans come unsalted, rinsing the canned beans for one minute in cold water will wash away a quarter of the sodium.
- **Buy low-sodium beans**: If you're watching your salt intake (and you should be), purchase canned low-sodium beans. Once you use the cold water trick, you've significantly decreased the amount of salt you're ingesting.
- **Buy vegetarian beans**: Baked and refried varieties are traditionally prepared with lard or pork, which add calories, cholesterol, sodium, and saturated fat, none of which you want to add into your diet. A healthier alternative is vegetarian refried beans. They contain no saturated fat and have 2 more grams of protein than the nonvegetarian ones.

62. Catch Some Tuna

It's not a coincidence that 90 percent of all bodybuilders and fitness competitors in the world will tell you they make a habit of feasting on tuna. They know it's an excellent source of protein that offers very few calories and almost no fat. These people need to be lean to compete, and tuna is often their answer. Caution: Eat tuna in moderation (once or twice a week) because it can be high in mercury. Alternate it with other fish, such as salmon.

63. Combine Protein with Carbohydrates

Protein and carbohydrates are meant to go together. Protein helps your body process carbohydrates by slowing down the absorption of sugars and tamping down the production of excess insulin. Eating healthy complex carbohydrates with protein will also help you eat less, particularly if you're eating high-calorie proteins. Try whole-grain crackers with cheese, yogurt with fruit, or a glass of milk with oatmeal.

CHAPTER 5

Boost Your Metabolism by . . .

INCREASING FIBER CONSUMPTION

64. Bulk Up with Fiber

Nutritionally speaking, fiber is the indigestible part of food you eat—the stuff that passes through your digestive system relatively quickly and intact, such as the bran in grain, the pulp in fruit, and the skin of certain vegetables such as corn. By traveling so quickly, it also rushes other foods through your system, giving cancer-causing compounds less time to do their dirty work, and moving excess calories through your system before they turn into fat, which keeps your metabolic rate high. Fiber also promotes healthy digestion by stimulating the action of beneficial bacteria and dilutes potential carcinogens, reducing their ability to do harm. A diet high in fiber will fill you up so you're less likely to eat unhealthy foods that slow down your metabolism, and it will help you maintain healthy cholesterol and blood sugar levels, making it a great tool for weight management.

65. Know Your Fibers

There are four major types of fiber, and each can benefit your body in a special way:

1. **Cellulose**. The most common type of fiber is found in most fruits and vegetables, as well as in whole grains and some types of nuts. Cellulose is an effective stool softener and helps dilute bile acids in the colon, which are believed to stimulate the growth of certain types of cancer.
2. **Gums**. These sticky fibers are derived from plants. They help lower cholesterol and may help prevent certain types of cancer, though researchers are still trying to figure out exactly how they work. Gums are found in oat bran, dried beans, and oatmeal and are commonly used to thicken processed foods.

3. **Lignin**. This fiber acts as a binder for cellulose and is found in certain fruits, nuts, peas, tomatoes, and whole grains. It doesn't have the same action as cellulose on stools or bile acids, but laboratory studies have shown that it can help prevent the onset of cancer.

4. **Pectin**. This gelatinous compound supplements the action of cellulose. It helps limit the potential damage from bile acids and also aids digestion by preventing diarrhea. Rich sources of pectin include apples, bananas, beets, carrots, and a wide array of citrus fruit.

66. Know Why Soluble Fiber Is Great for Your Metabolism

Soluble fiber plays two important roles: (1) It binds to bile as it travels through your small intestine, and (2) it helps keep blood sugar levels manageable. Since bile acids assist fat digestion and allow cholesterol to stick around, the faster soluble fiber ushers fat through your system, the less fat and cholesterol you retain. And the steadier your blood sugar levels are, the more efficient your metabolic process remains.

Foods containing soluble fiber include:

- Oat/oat bran
- Dried beans and peas
- Nuts
- Barley
- Flaxseed
- Fruits such as oranges and apples
- Vegetables such as carrots
- Psyllium husk

67. Know Why Insoluble Fiber Is Great for Your Metabolism

Insoluble fiber does not dissolve as it travels through your digestive system. The benefits of insoluble fiber are twofold: (1) It creates a feeling of fullness that help you eat less, and (2) it speeds things along and lessens the amount of fats, cholesterol, sugars, and starches that are absorbed. One caveat: Too much insoluble fiber may have a deleterious effect if it prevents absorption of nutrients.

Foods containing insoluble fiber include:

- Corn bran
- Vegetables such as green beans and dark green leafy vegetables
- Seeds and nuts
- Fruit skins and root vegetable skins
- Whole-wheat products

68. Check Your Fiber Consumption

Despite efforts by government health agencies to boost fiber intake, the typical American still consumes an average of only 11 grams of fiber each day. According to the National Cancer Institute, an amount double that would be far more beneficial. Studies have shown that consuming between 20 and 30 grams of fiber a day can dramatically reduce your risk for many cancers. Look at the fiber content on the Nutrition Facts Label on packaged foods. Good sources of fiber have at least 2.5 grams of fiber per serving.

Consuming more than that, however, can cause painful and embarrassing bloating and flatulence. To avoid these problems, introduce fiber into your diet gradually and try to get as much as you can from the foods you eat, rather than relying on fiber supplements.

69. Always Choose High-Fiber Grains over Processed Grains

We all know by now that white bread, white rice, and plain crackers contain a lot of empty calories and a lot less fiber than whole-grain breads, cereals, crackers, and rice. One of the quickest and healthiest ways to boost your fiber intake—and thereby your metabolism—is to substitute higher-fiber foods, such as whole-grain breads, crackers, or chips, brown rice, and whole-wheat pasta for lower-fiber foods, such as white bread, white rice, or plain crackers.

70. Eat More Raw Vegetables

Fresh vegetables provide plenty of fiber, but cooking vegetables can reduce their fiber content. Plus, the vegetables will retain more of their nutrients if you undercook them, and even more if you eat them raw. Eating raw vegetables—sans butter or oil—is very low in fat, and will fill you up, thus helping you cut back on foods that will be difficult to metabolize.

71. Savor These Fiber-Filled Vegetables

Consume a variety of vegetables to obtain different sources of fiber. Mature vegetables (those harvested at later growth stages) tend to contain more lignin; those harvested at an earlier growth stage have higher contents of pectin and hemicellulose. Eat as much as you want of these vegetables without feeling guilty: asparagus, beets, broccoli, cabbage, carrots, cauliflower, celery, chicory, chili peppers, cucumber, dandelion, endive, garden cress, garlic, green beans, lettuce, onions, radishes, spinach, and turnips.

72. Eschew Juice for Fruit

Fruits are also fabulous sources of fiber, but most of the fiber in fruit is found in the skin and pulp, which is removed when the juice is made. Juice can also contain too many concentrated calories, particularly sugars that will slow metabolism. Keep in mind that citrus fruits may add a little additional heat to your metabolic furnace.

73. Savor These Fiber-Filled Fruits

Try eating different fruits every day to get different types of dietary fiber. Fruits with edible seeds, such as strawberries, are sources of lignin, while apples and citrus fruits are excellent sources of pectin. One medium apple contains 4.4 grams of fiber, and one cup of strawberries contains 3 grams. These other fiber-filled fruits will also help boost your metabolism: bananas, blueberries, cantaloupes, cranberries, grapefruits, honeydew melons, lemons, limes, mangos, oranges, papayas, peaches, pineapples, raspberries, tomatoes, tangerines, and watermelons.

74. Eat Fiber-Rich Cereals

Start your day with a high-fiber breakfast cereal, such as bran cereal or oatmeal. Cereals offer an excellent source of healthy fiber, and often they are fortified with vitamins. Look for cereals that contain at least 5 grams of fiber per serving because the more fiber it contains, the longer and harder your metabolism will have to burn to digest it. Add fresh fruit for an extra fiber boost.

75. Find Other Ways to Add Fiber to Your Diet

Adding fiber to your diet may be easier than you think. Here are some additional tips that can help you get started:

- Plan to eat high-fiber foods such as fruits, vegetables, legumes, or whole-grain starches at every meal.
- Eat a variety of high-fiber foods to ensure you get a mix of both types of fiber.
- Use snacks to increase your fiber intake by nibbling on higher-fiber foods, such as dried fruits, popcorn, fresh fruit, raw vegetables, or whole-wheat crackers.
- Try to eat legumes, or dried beans, at least two to three times per week. Add them to salads, soups, casseroles, or spaghetti sauce.

76. Eat an Apple

Apples are fabulous for you—and your metabolism. The active ingredient in apple pulp is pectin, a soluble form of fiber that helps reduce "bad" cholesterol by keeping it in the intestinal tract until it is eliminated. Pectin also creates a sensation of fullness and suppresses appetite. A study published in the *Journal of the National Cancer Institute* shows that pectin binds certain cancer-causing compounds in the colon, accelerating their removal from the body. European studies indicate that apple pectin can even help eliminate lead, mercury, and other toxic heavy metals from the human body. Note: It's important to wash apples thoroughly and to avoid eating the seeds, which can be poisonous. All apples provide super nutrients, but eating different varieties of apples is even better.

77. Eat Your Oatmeal

Oatmeal is a marvelous choice for healthy fiber, both soluble and insoluble. Insoluble fiber found in oatmeal is good for people with diabetes because the fibers slow down the digestion of starch, preventing a sharp rise in blood glucose levels after a meal. Soluble fiber aids in the processing and elimination of food, moving it quickly and efficiently through the bowels. Studies have shown that eating foods that are high in soluble fiber may help to lower LDL cholesterol (bad cholesterol) without lowering HDL cholesterol (good cholesterol). Whether you choose steel-cut oats (the most roughly cut and least processed), rolled or "old-fashioned" oats, quick oats, or instant, all types of oats are effective at reducing cholesterol. To get the daily 3 grams of soluble fiber recommended for lowering cholesterol levels, you'll need to eat 2 ounces of oat bran (⅔ cup dry or about 1½ cups cooked) or 3 ounces of oatmeal (1 cup dry or 2 cups cooked).

78. Have an Occasional Fiber-Filled Day

If you want to lose a few pounds quickly, spend a few days eating only fiber-filled foods like fruits and vegetables. Be sure to drink plenty of water and try not to exceed 30 grams of fiber in one day to avoid gastrointestinal discomfort. The healthiest choice, of course, is to make sure every day is a fiber-filled day with plenty of fruits and vegetables in addition to whole grains, lean proteins, and healthy fats. This will fill you up, crank up your metabolism, and keep you from eating more calorie-laden foods

CHAPTER 6
Boost Your Metabolism by . . .
ADOPTING HEALTHY EATING HABITS

Do the Opposite of What You Normally Do

Eat Carbohydrates Early in the Day

Always Break Your Fast Shortly after Rising

Eat a High-Fiber Breakfast to Lower Fat Consumption

Don't Skip Meals

Keep Your Blood Sugar Stable

Avoid Social Eating

Just Say No at the Movies

Ditto for Ballparks

Avoid French Fries

Say No to White Sauce

Avoid Thick-Crust Pizza

Don't Go Overboard on Vacations

Trade Traditional Pasta for Spaghetti Squash

Don't Shop When Hungry

Avoid the Most Dangerous Aisle in the Supermarket

Shop the Perimeters

Plan Your Meals Ahead of Time

Eat Less

Eat Enough

Eat Several Small Meals a Day

Stop Eating Before You Feel Full

79. Do the Opposite of What You Normally Do

If you are seeking ways to boost your metabolism, struggling with weight issues, and want to improve your overall health, it's important to adopt healthy eating habits. To do this, you may need to take a close look at the way you're eating and decide to overhaul your lifestyle. Make the decision to make the following changes—and watch your metabolism skyrocket as a result!

80. Eat Carbohydrates Early in the Day

As carbohydrates are easily metabolized into fat, eat the bulk of your carbohydrates early in the day so your body will have plenty of time to metabolize them. For example, rather than eating a light breakfast and a heavy dinner, eat your heaviest meal for breakfast and your lightest meal at dinnertime. Doing so will not only get your engine going in the morning, you will metabolize the bulk of your daily calories when you're most active. Help your body burn carbohydrate calories by exercising in the morning or making special efforts to walk throughout the day. Obviously, a body in motion burns more calories than a body at rest.

81. Always Break Your Fast Shortly after Rising

After you've slept for eight hours, breakfast breaks that fast. When you do so, you pump up your metabolism by flooding your body with food that your body breaks down into blood sugar—also known as glucose—which your body uses as energy. As a result, those who eat breakfast (as opposed to those who skip it) find it easier to concentrate, solve problems, and have more strength and endurance for activity because their muscles are dining on the glucose that's just been deposited into the bloodstream. Here are some healthy suggestions to enjoy in the morning:

- Cold cereal with fruit and skim milk
- Bran muffin and a banana
- Hard-boiled egg and grapefruit juice
- Yogurt with fruit or low-fat granola cereal
- Peanut butter on whole-wheat toast and an orange
- Instant oatmeal with raisins or berries
- Breakfast smoothie (blend fruit and skim milk)
- Low-fat cottage cheese and peaches

82. Eat a High-Fiber Breakfast to Lower Fat Consumption

If you think breakfasts are unhealthy, maybe you need to rethink what you're eating. A doughnut and coffee aren't going to start your day off right, but what about eggs, whole-wheat toast, and a small salad or piece of fruit? By eating a high-fiber breakfast, you can stay fuller for longer, and it will help you not reach for that sugary snack in the office kitchen or in the pantry. Research has shown that eating a high-fiber, low-fat breakfast can result in a lower fat intake for the entire day, which helps your metabolism because it can use the fat already stored in your body for energy. If you can't stand the thought of eating breakfast, start out with something like toast or fruit and bring a snack with you for later in the morning when you get hungry.

83. Don't Skip Meals

One of the worst things you can to your metabolism is skip meals. By doing so, you slow your metabolism. Your body thinks it is going into starvation mode and needs to conserve energy by storing fat, even though you're trying to lose weight. Aggravating, we know. But also consider that by skipping one potentially healthy meal, you may later overeat and throw off your day's calorie intake altogether. So, instead of skipping meals, do the opposite—eat well-balanced meals and snack on healthy foods throughout the day. This will help boost your metabolism instead of bringing it to a standstill.

84. Keep Your Blood Sugar Stable

In addition to the types of fuel you put into your body, your energy can be directly linked to the amount of energy you put (or don't put) into your body and the timing of it. Nutrition, as you know, is all about fueling the body for optimum function. Many Americans have become so preoccupied with weight loss that they have lost sight of the main event: You need food and glucose—the energy source found in food—to live. If you don't give your body glucose through balanced meals, your metabolism will slow down and your sugar cravings will increase. When blood sugar dips too low, your brain thinks it's starving. This is why you end up craving high-sugar foods; since most high-sugar foods are also high-fat foods, desperation eating packs a double caloric whammy. Well-timed and well-balanced meals will boost your metabolism because you won't be hungry as often, making you less likely to reach for non-nutritious foods.

BOOST YOUR METABOLISM BY . . . **ADOPTING HEALTHY EATING HABITS**

85. Avoid Social Eating

We are all at our most vulnerable when eating in social situations. At parties, after one cocktail in the midst of conversation, we'll find ourselves accepting hors d'oeuvres one after another, and then eating whatever is put on our plates, including dessert. To spare yourself, eat healthy food, especially protein, before you go to the party, and then stick to nonalcoholic, low-calorie beverages. This will lower your susceptibility to eat or drink more than you intend. It is possible to avoid social eating, but it takes a lot of discipline and commitment to health. Find what works for you, and go with it.

86. Just Say No at the Movies

Gobbling up obscene amounts of fat and calories has become a sad tradition in movie theaters. When you go to a movie, your best bet is to skip those snacks entirely. Except for an occasional soft pretzel, there are virtually zero healthy options at a theater—and most are ridiculously unhealthy and massively fattening. Smuggle in something healthy like dried fruit, baked chips, or veggie sticks, or choose to find satisfaction with two hours of entertainment.

87. Ditto for Ballparks

Never plan to eat a meal at a sporting event. Ballparks are synonymous with garbage food, and it's a bad idea to be stuck there starving while surrounded by lukewarm pizzas, hot dogs, and nachos. Instead, eat a healthy meal before you go. If you must have a snack, stick to a soft pretzel or a sorbet.

88. Avoid French Fries

A 130-pound woman would have to run 3 miles at 6 miles per hour in order to burn off the calories in a medium order of McDonald's French fries. Note we said "medium," not an order of large fries. Wouldn't it be easier to skip the French fries altogether? You can easily consume lots of calories; burning off lots of calories is hard work!

89. Say No to White Sauce

Traditional Alfredo is the worst of all sauces. It's the perfect combination of butter, cream, and cheese, which leads to a caloric and fat count nightmare. If flat abs are on your to-do list, do not order this at a restaurant. Marinara will always be a better bet!

90. Avoid Thick-Crust Pizza

Pizza has the potential to be really good or really bad for you. The power is in your hands. When making or ordering pizza, make sure you always choose the thinnest crust possible while piling on lean meats and fresh or grilled produce. To maximize nutrition and minimize fat, ask them to merely sprinkle cheese on top (rather than slathering on two handfuls of cheese).

91. Don't Go Overboard on Vacations

Vacations are designed for people to get away from the daily grind, see something new, and have some fun. They are not designed for people to blow their healthy habits and gain ten pounds as quickly as possible.

Always include exercise as part of your day wherever you are and stick with healthy eating habits.

92. Trade Traditional Pasta for Spaghetti Squash

Almost everyone loves pasta! But, unfortunately, traditional pasta has a heavy caloric pricetag. The good news for all you spaghetti lovers out there is that spaghetti squash is the perfect substitution for pasta. It has a mild flavor, tastes great with tomato sauce, and twirls like spaghetti! This versatile squash can be baked, boiled, microwaved, or cooked in a Crock Pot! One cup of spaghetti squash contains only 42 calories and 0.4 grams of fat. Its benefits include 2.2 grams of fiber per cup in addition to a bounty of nutrients like vitamin A, folic acid, and potassium.

93. Don't Shop When Hungry

Grocery shopping when hungry frequently leads to impulse purchases that contain more fat and calories than you would choose if you shopped when satiated. One of the best ways to boost your metabolism is to plan meals ahead of time, create a shopping list, and adhere to the list when you shop. This way, you're far more likely to make healthier food choices.

94. Avoid the Most Dangerous Aisle in the Supermarket

Avoid the bakery aisle at all cost! In the past, trans fat was commonly used in baked goods because it made them soft and flaky, contributed to a delicious flavor and mouth-feel, was inexpensive, and extended the shelf life of the product. However, due to regulations passed by the Food and Drug Administration (FDA), all packaged goods are now required to list the amount of trans fat per serving and many companies have elected to cut back on the amount of trans fat used in their products as a result of this disclosure.

Be careful though. Companies are only required to list the amount of trans fat per serving, and they don't have to list anything under 0.5 grams. That means if you eat more than the recommended serving—a metabolism don't on any day—you could be eating a dangerous amount of trans fat.

Some items in the bakery may not be labeled, but you can ask the bakery manager for nutrition information. If she doesn't have it, then ask to see the ingredient list for your favorite products. If that list includes the words *hydrogenated* or *shortening*, then you know that the bread, cookie, or pastry contains artificial trans fat.

95. Shop the Perimeters

One of the best ways to make the healthiest food selections is to shop the perimeters of your grocery store. Most grocery stores house the produce, dairy products, protein, and fresh food on the perimeter aisles. All those aisles in the middle house processed foods, snacks, cookies, ice cream, soda, and sugary cereals. Next to making a list and sticking to it, avoiding aisles where temptation might lure you into buying unhealthy foods is the most important thing you can do to boost your metabolism.

96. Plan Your Meals Ahead of Time

Obviously, planning your meals long before you eat will help you make smarter food choices and balance your diet. Start by planning for one day, then two, and so on until you are planning a week or two ahead. That way, you can select the variety of foods needed to provide maximum nutrition and take advantage of all the food tips in this book that will help you boost your metabolism.

The famed Mayo Clinic's website (*www.mayoclinic.com*) provides a calculator for an individualized "Healthy Weight Pyramid." Enter your info for a customized pyramid that will help you plan your meals for maximum nutrition and health benefits. Then, take their advice, as follows:

- Plan healthy meals and snacks using recommended food servings. Focus on foods at the base of the pyramid—fruits, vegetables, and whole grains.
- Be familiar with the serving sizes in each food group.
- Spread out the food servings throughout the day. Include at least one serving from most food groups at each meal.
- Stay flexible and adjust your food-serving goals as necessary. If, for example, you don't reach your fruit goal on Monday, add extra servings of fruit to Tuesday's menu.

97. Eat Less

The basic methodology behind losing weight is simple—burn more than you consume. To lose a pound of fat in a week, you need to create a deficit of 3,500 calories. You can achieve this by reducing your normal food intake by 500 calories, by burning 500 extra calories each day, or through a combination of the two.

98. Eat Enough

It's extremely common for people who are dieting to eat too little. You will lose weight to start, but your body won't understand that you have plenty of food but are choosing to minimize the intake of calories. Instead, your body notices that supply has gone way down, deduces that you don't have enough food available to eat, and lowers your metabolism to burn what you do eat more slowly. It also hoards extra fat in case your energy reserves go too low. Instead of depriving your body, keep your metabolism high by eating around 1,200 calories a day. If you do this, your body should continue burning fat and you'll continue to lose weight.

99. Eat Several Small Meals a Day

The act of eating and digesting burns calories, so every time you eat, your metabolism kicks in. If you eat small meals spaced throughout the day, you'll be firing up the furnace every two to three hours. Once lit, your metabolic fires will burn until the fuel runs dry, so making sure your body has a constant supply of fuel is an ideal way to boost your metabolism. That said, it's important that you limit what you eat to healthy food in healthy portions. Also, combining protein with a complex carb and a healthy fat is ideal, just make low-calorie choices and keep those home fires burning.

100. Stop Eating Before You Feel Full

It takes at least 20 minutes for your stomach to let your brain know that you're full. Slowing down will give your body time to alert you before it's 100 percent full, and it will give you the option to knowingly and willingly cut back on the amount of food you eat. Eat only when you are truly hungry and stop when you're satisfied. Eating more slowly also ensures proper digestion. To slow down, take sips of your beverage between bites, put your fork down, and enjoy the conversation of others. Sit down to eat instead of eating while standing, driving, or watching television. Eating while doing other things means you are eating unconsciously and can easily consume more.

CHAPTER 7

Boost Your Metabolism by . . .

EATING SUPERFOODS

Add Superfoods to Your Diet

Eat Nutrient-Rich Vegetables

Love Those Omegas

Eat Flax

Eat a Nut

Eat Walnuts in Particular

Munch on Pumpkin Seeds

Eat a Sweet Potato

Eat Asparagus

Eat Quinoa

Pile on the Garlic

Eat Parsley

Try Sea Vegetables

Consume Micro-plants

Chomp on Chives

Munch on Olives

Eat More Wild Salmon

Eat Fresh Blueberries

Eat Avocados

Feast on Low-Fat Yogurt

Eat Dark Chocolate

101. Add Superfoods to Your Diet

Superfoods are natural foods that are nutritive powerhouses. They work to ensure your body gets what it needs to be healthy. Loaded with nutrients, superfoods can help you lower your cholesterol, reduce your risk of heart disease and cancer, stabilize your moods, and more importantly, boost your metabolism. According to nutritionist Elizabeth Somer, author of *The Essential Guide to Vitamins and Minerals*, a healthy diet incorporating a variety of the superfoods discussed in this chapter will help you maintain your weight, fight disease, and live longer. One thing these foods all have in common? "Every superfood is going to be a 'real' (unprocessed) food," Somer points out. "You don't find fortified potato chips in the superfood category."

102. Eat Nutrient-Rich Vegetables

Everyone knows that vegetables are good for us, but some vegetables are healthier than others and can help metabolism. In fact, many vegetables will satisfy—or nearly satisfy—your daily requirements for several vitamins. From dark leafy greens rich in calcium, iron, and magnesium to the cruciferous vegetables like bok choy, broccoli, cabbage, turnips, and water cress that have cancer-preventing antioxidants to nutrient-rich vegetables like carrots, potatoes, yams, and tomatoes, vegetables are always a good thing to snack on and include with each meal.

103. Love Those Omegas

Omega-3 fatty acids are great for promoting heart health because they protect against deadly arrhythmias by making the heart cells more stable and less prone to overexcitement. In one study, those who ate fish just once or twice a week were 40 percent less likely to die suddenly from a cardiac arrhythmia. In addition, omega-3 fatty acids may decrease the risk of a stroke, and they are excellent at maintaining good blood sugar levels. Studies have even suggested that they may play a factor in weight loss. Thus, it's important to make sure they're a staple of your healthy diet. Omega-3 fatty acids can be found in wild salmon, mackerel, herring, dried butternuts, black walnuts, soybeans, sardines, lake trout, Chinook salmon, cooked pinto beans, fortified eggs, flaxseed, and walnuts. These superfoods also have the added benefit of being high in monounsaturated fats, which can lower cholesterol.

104. Eat Flax

Loaded with omega-3 fatty acids, flax bolsters cell membranes and helps your body respond more efficiently to insulin, thereby improving glucose absorption, which in turn helps stabilize blood sugar levels. In other words, flax is one superfood you can easily incorporate in your diet and reap major metabolic benefits. You can buy flaxseed oil at most supermarkets or health food stores, or toss ground flaxseeds (if they aren't ground, they don't provide the same benefits) on your granola or oatmeal. Flax is also readily available in many types of bread; just check the ingredients!

105. Eat a Nut

Nuts are high in fat, but they contain minerals, fiber, and nice amounts of protein. All nuts and seeds are small powerhouses. They are so powerful, in fact, that just having a serving of nuts five times a week can significantly reduce your risk for heart disease. However, nuts are high in calories and should be eaten in moderation; think of a serving as a tablespoon or two. Look for nuts that are unsalted; it's not important whether they are roasted or unroasted. Nuts are great sprinkled on foods high in vitamin C, such as fruit and vegetables, because the vitamin C increases the body's absorption of the iron in nuts.

106. Eat Walnuts in Particular

The walnut is the only nut that provides significant amounts of alpha-linolenic acid, one of the three omega-3 fatty acids. Because your body cannot produce this acid, it needs to be provided daily from other sources. Seven walnuts can fulfill your daily need for these essential fatty acids. Omega-3s are brain food. Their high amounts of unsaturated fat help lower LDL or "bad" cholesterol in your blood and increase HDL, the "good" cholesterol. By eating a handful of walnuts a day, you can also reduce your risk for heart disease.

107. Munch on Pumpkin Seeds

Pumpkin seeds, also known as pepitas, nestle in the core of the pumpkin encased in a white-yellow husk. This superseed contains a number of minerals such as zinc, magnesium, manganese, iron, copper, and phosphorus, along with proteins, monounsaturated fat, and the omega fatty acids 3 and 6—all of which will help boost your metabolism. Today the superpowers of pumpkin seeds have been found to help prevent prostate cancer in men, protect against heart disease, and have anti-inflammatory benefits.

108. Eat a Sweet Potato

Sweet potatoes have high amounts of beta-carotene, equal to that of carrots; for only 90 calories per sweet potato, you get a huge amount of health-building nutrients. Beta-carotene is a major fighter against cancer, heart disease, asthma, and rheumatoid arthritis. The bright orange flesh contains carotenoids that help boost your metabolism, stabilize your blood sugar, and lower insulin resistance, which makes your cells more responsive to insulin. Sweet potatoes have four times the Recommended Dietary Allowance for beta-carotene when eaten with the skin on. In fact, it would take 20 cups of broccoli to provide the amount of beta-carotene (vitamin A) available in a cup of cooked sweet potatoes. They are a source of vitamin E, vitamin B6, potassium, and iron, and have even been found to provide as much fiber as oatmeal. Plus they're fat-free! Sweet potatoes are definitely a superfood!

109. Eat Asparagus

This vegetable is easy to cook and is a heart-healthy source of vitamins A, C, and K. In addition, it also contains the carbohydrate inulin, which promotes the growth and activity of good bacteria in your intestines. Pregnant women can especially benefit from its high folate levels, which help prevent birth defects.

110. Eat Quinoa

Once known as "the gold of the Incas," this grain—a complete protein—includes all nine essential amino acids, making it an excellent choice for vegetarians, vegans, and everyone else as well! Quinoa has extra-high

BOOST YOUR METABOLISM BY . . . **EATING SUPERFOODS**

amounts of the amino acid lysine, which is essential for tissue growth and repair. Combine this protein with quinoa's high amounts of potassium and its magnesium content to help lower your blood pressure and strengthen your heart. For such a small grain, quinoa not only provides a whole lot of nutrients and helps boost your metabolism, but it may also be especially valuable for people with migraine headaches, diabetes, atherosclerosis, and other debilitating health issues. It is also a very good source of manganese as well as magnesium, iron, copper, phosphorus, and B vitamins.

111. Pile on the Garlic

Garlic, one of the world's most popular culinary herbs, has a long history as a medicinal plant. Indeed, scientific studies have verified what herbalists have known for centuries—that garlic both prevents and treats illness in a wide variety of ways.

Among its many attributes, garlic is known to lower cholesterol levels, thin the blood, kill bacteria, boost the immune system, lower blood sugar levels, reduce the risk of certain types of cancer, and fire up the metabolic furnace. There is also evidence that the herb helps relieve asthma, eases ear infections, and facilitates healthy cell function. Bottom line: Those who wish to maintain their health and age well should eat lots of garlic.

Incorporate fresh garlic into salads by chopping, crushing, or putting it through a garlic press (2 or 3 cloves a day is optimum). Whole garlic bulbs can be oven roasted and the individual cloves can be squeezed out onto bread or toast as a creamy spread. If you decide to take garlic capsules, take 1 to 3 capsules daily, or follow the label directions. Garlic has blood-thinning properties so, if you're taking it in supplement form, tell your doctor before surgery and use caution when using antiplatelet or blood-thinning medications.

112. Eat Parsley

Parsley is loaded with compounds that purify your blood and expel toxins from your body. It is also dense in vitamin C, vitamin A, vitamin K, iodine, iron, and chlorophyll. Actually, parsley has higher vitamin C content than citrus and is an excellent ingredient to battle inflammation. It also contains certain volatile oils that have been shown to inhibit the formation of tumors, particularly in the lungs. Parsley is also rich in flavonoids known for their antioxidant activity and helps prevent free radical damage (a major metabolism buster) to your body's cells. Parsley's dark green color also provides needed oxygenating chlorophyll, which increases the antioxidant capacity of your blood.

113. Try Sea Vegetables

Gram for gram, sea vegetables—seaweeds and algae—are higher in essential vitamins and minerals than any other known food group. These minerals are bio-available to the body in chelated, colloidal forms that make them more easily absorbed. Sea vegetables that provide minerals in this colloidal form have been shown to retain their molecular identity while remaining in liquid suspension. The following is a descriptive list of what sea vegetables can add to your daily diet:

- They can contain as much as 48 percent protein.
- They are a rich source of both soluble and insoluble dietary fiber.

BOOST YOUR METABOLISM BY . . . **EATING SUPERFOODS**

- The brown sea varieties—kelp, wakame, and kombu—contain alginic acid, which has been shown to remove heavy metals and radioactive isotopes from the digestive tract.
- They contain significant amounts of vitamin A, in the form of beta-carotene, as well as vitamins B, C, and E.
- They are high in potassium, calcium, sodium, iron, and chloride.
- They provide the fifty-six minerals and trace minerals that your body requires to function properly.

114. Consume Micro-plants

Micro-plants consisting of blue-green algae, chlorella, spirulina, wheat grass, and barley grass contain more vitamins and minerals than kale and broccoli. They are an excellent source of two important phytochemicals: chlorophyll and lycopene. Micro-plants, commercially known as green foods, contain a concentrated combination of phytochemicals, vitamins, minerals, bioflavonoids, proteins, amino acids, essential fatty acids, enzymes, coenzymes, and fiber. They support your body's ability to detoxify heavy metals, pesticides, and other toxins, plus boost your immunity to disease.

115. Chomp on Chives

Chives and chive flowers are high in vitamin C, folic acid, potassium, calcium, and blood-building iron. They promote good digestion, reduce flatulence, prevent bad breath, and help stimulate your metabolism. Chives, when eaten regularly, may help to lower blood cholesterol levels. Because of their high vitamin C content, they may help speed recovery from a cold; the sulfurous compounds contained in chives are natural expectorants. Best used fresh, chives are easy to grow in pots at home.

116. Munch on Olives

Long an essential part of the Mediterranean diet, olives are delicious, and their oil, high in monounsaturated fats, has been in the news because of its ability to reduce "bad" cholesterol in the blood. Researchers also suspect olive oil may protect against gastrointestinal cancer by influencing the metabolism of the gut. Olive oil also contains Vitamin E, antioxidants, and beta-carotene—all metabolism boosters. Dr. Andrew Weil recommends the exclusive use of olive oil for fat in the diet. Studies have shown that people who consume olive oil in preference to other fats have a lower incidence of heart disease.

117. Eat More Wild Salmon

Salmon is one of the primary superfoods. That's because it's laden with two types of omega-3 fatty acids (DHA and EPA) that can have a dramatic impact on reducing heart disease, Alzheimer's disease, Parkinson's disease, and osteoporosis. With their anti-inflammatory properties, these fatty acids also help blood clots from forming unnecessarily within the circulatory system, may even prevent cardiac arrhythmia, and may help calm an overactive immune system in people with autoimmune diseases. For the healthiest, most eco-friendly, nutrient-packed salmon, check your grocery or local farmers' market for wild salmon.

118. Eat Fresh Blueberries

In a *Newsweek* article dated June 17, 2002, neuroscientist James Joseph of Tufts University made it clear that when it comes to brain protection, there's nothing quite like the blueberry. Dr. Joseph calls it the "brain berry" and attributes its health benefits to antioxidant and anti-inflammatory compounds. He sees potential for reversing short-term memory loss and forestalling many other effects of aging. The American Institute for Cancer Research recommends eating blueberries because they are "one of the best sources of antioxidants, substances that can slow the aging process and reduce cell damage that can lead to cancer." By eating only half a cup of fresh or frozen blueberries a day, you can receive their antioxidant protection and benefit from their anti-aging and metabolism-boosting properties. When out of season, use frozen blueberries in a smoothie or mixed with yogurt and walnuts as a delicious snack.

119. Eat Avocados

Avocados are incredibly healthful for you. In addition to being packed with important vitamins, avocados are able to lower bad cholesterol, decrease your risk for cancer, and prevent heart disease because they include oleic acid (a monounsaturated fat) and healthy fatty acids, and they are high in magnesium and potassium. Research has also shown that these tasty fruits help the body absorb nutrients from other foods eaten with them. Just keep in mind that an avocado is high in calories—each fruit contains approximately 300 calories and 35 grams of fat—as you figure out new ways to incorporate it into your meals.

120. Feast on Low-Fat Yogurt

Yogurt is tasty and a great source of protein and calcium—which we'll touch on soon—but some yogurt also comes loaded with live cultures known as probiotics. These creatures live in your intestine and are warriors against bad bacteria and help with the digestive process (a recent study showed that people who ate three servings of light yogurt a day lost 20 percent more weight than those who reduced their calorie intake alone).

121. Eat Dark Chocolate

Chocolate is good for you. Well, sort of. It's still high in calories, but an ounce of dark chocolate will provide you with antioxidants and can help lower your blood pressure. Just keep in mind that the darker the chocolate, the better off you are because dark chocolate contains the least amount of fat and sugar.

CHAPTER 8
Boost Your Metabolism by . . .
DRINKING IT UP

122. Stay Hydrated

The liquids you consume have a powerful impact on your metabolism. Some will help it, while others will make it sluggish and may even lead to unhealthy weight gain. In this chapter, we'll discuss the best beverages to boost your metabolism. However, the best drink for your body—even if you drink nothing else—is water. Water, which makes up 55–75 percent of our bodies, regulates body temperature, transports nutrients, carries waste away from cells, protects the organs from damage, and keeps you hydrated. Water is also necessary to keep the metabolic processes functioning and helps you expel waste by adding fluid to the stool so you don't become constipated. And, in some studies, it's been found that after you drink a pint of water, your metabolism revs up and burns 25 calories. So, as we go through this chapter, keep in mind that while you may want to try out some of the suggestions here, water should be an integral part of each day's diet.

123. Know How Much Water You Need

The body has no provision to store water. Therefore, the amount of water lost each day must be continually replaced to maintain good health and proper body function. On average, we lose about 10 cups of water each day just through perspiration, breathing, urination, and bowel movements. This does not include hot days or days when you exercise and perspire even more. To avoid dehydration, the body needs an ongoing supply of water throughout the day; the average adult needs 8 to 12 cups of water each day. By the time you feel thirsty, you can already be on your way to becoming dehydrated. To be sure you are properly hydrated, check your urine to make sure it is diluted or clear rather than a darker yellow.

124. Drink Everything on the Rocks

Whenever feasible, add ice cubes to your drinks. When you drink ice-cold beverages, your body fires up its furnace to warm the water for maximum absorption. Five or six glasses of water, with ice cubes, may burn up an extra 10 calories a day, which could add up to a pound per year.

125. Have a Few Cups of Java

Caffeine stimulates your central nervous system, digestive tract, and your metabolism. Researchers studied a 145-pound woman who consumed 2 cups of coffee a day. They found that in the four hours after drinking the coffee, she burned an extra 50 calories. That said, adding cream and sugar will add calories and fat that will diffuse coffee's metabolic benefits, and drinking too much coffee can be detrimental to your overall health. Drinking 1 to 2 small cups of coffee in the morning, with breakfast, is just enough to get your metabolic furnace burning.

126. Drink Iced Coffee

Why not kill two birds with one stone and drink your coffee with ice? This way, you get all the metabolic benefits of a normal cup of joe with an icy added boost! To make sure your ice-cold coffee is really boosting your metabolism, drink it black or with skim milk, and avoid adding sugar.

127. Limit Caffeine

It is important to remember that caffeine is a drug, one that is absorbed quickly in the body and can raise blood pressure, heart rate, and brain serotonin levels (low levels of serotonin cause drowsiness). Withdrawal from caffeine can cause headaches and drowsiness. The pharmacologically active dose of caffeine is defined as 200 milligrams, and the daily recommended, not-to-exceed intake level is the equivalent of 1 to 3 cups of coffee per day (139 to 417 milligrams). Too much caffeine also tricks you into thinking you don't need more sleep. Lack of sleep can prevent your metabolism from working normally and increase the level of cortisol released, which increases hunger. Here is a guideline for approximate amounts of caffeine in commonly used foods and beverages:

Beverage	Serving Amount	Amount of Caffeine (mg)
Coffee, brewed from ground beans	6 oz.	100
Coffee, instant	6 oz.	65
Tea, brewed from whole leaves	6 oz.	10–50
Cola, can or bottle	12 oz.	50
Cocoa, breakfast type	6 oz.	13
Cocoa, as milk chocolate bar	1 oz.	6
Guarana, tablet or capsule	800 mg	30
Maté, brewed as tea	6 oz.	25–50
Semisweet chocolate chips	1 cup	92
Bittersweet chocolate chips	1 cup	18–30
Caffeine tablet, proprietary product	1 tablet	100–200

128. Drink Green or Oolong Tea

Green tea and oolong tea contain caffeine and catechins, which have been shown to boost metabolism for approximately two hours. Researchers say drinking 2 to 4 cups of green or oolong tea throughout the day may help you burn an extra 50 calories, which can lead to a 5-pound loss over a year—without any other change in your diet. Obviously, adding sugar or cream would counteract the positive effects. Also, avoid green tea beverages that have high-fructose corn syrup, as they are loaded with sugar and not good for your metabolism.

129. Swap Out White Wine for Red

Red wine, in moderation, can have quite the positive impact on your health. Studies have shown that red wine may inhibit the formation of fat cells and help prevent obesity by affecting the gene SIRT1. Red wine is rich in antioxidants that can help raise HDL ("good") cholesterol and protect against heart disease. Its antioxidants come in two forms—flavonoids and nonflavonoids. One of these nonflavonoids is resveratrol, which you can learn more about in entry 347.

130. Limit the Amount of Alcohol You Drink

Alcohol, just like soda, is full of empty calories because it contains no nutrients that can be stored for fuel. Plus, while the body is processing alcohol through the stomach and liver, it is unable to convert elements—glucose, fatty acids, amino acids—into energy, which means more food ends up stored as fat.

131. Try Concord Grape Juice

If you're looking for an alternative to red wine, with similar health benefits, try Concord grape juice. It is high in polyphenols, which have anti-inflammatory and antioxidant properties that help to increase your metabolic rate. A Tufts University study found that Concord grape juice helps increase memory and improve cognitive and motor function as we age. Other studies have shown that the juice helps maintain immune function, and lowers total cholesterol and blood pressure. Remember to keep portions reasonable (4 ounces) to avoid going overboard on calories.

132. Avoid Soda

The normal bloodstream contains a total of 4 teaspoons of blood sugar. When you drink a can of soda, roughly 10 teaspoons of table sugar are absorbed into your bloodstream, causing your blood-sugar level to rocket to an excessive level, setting off alarms in the pancreas, and causing a large amount of insulin to come out to deal with the excess blood sugar. Some sugar is quickly ushered into the cells, including brain cells, and the rest is stored in your fat cells. When all this is done, maybe in about an hour, your blood sugar may fall dramatically and low blood sugar occurs. A drop in blood sugar causes your body to crave sweets, which are definite metabolism busters. Just say no to soda to avoid rapid swings in blood sugar and consumption of excess empty calories.

133. Have a Cup of Coffee or Tea Before Workouts

Even though energy drink companies tout the benefits of energy drinks before, during, or after exercise, many contain sugar, and you don't need sugar or electrolytes to boost energy for a workout of an hour or less. Many athletes have found that drinking a cup of coffee or tea, with additional water, stimulates their metabolic rate. Try enjoying a cup of coffee or tea (about 200 mg of caffeine) prior to your exercise, and avoid high-potency caffeinated "turbo" drinks or pills. Check with your doctor if you are sensitive to caffeine. By the way, this does not mean drinking a latte or mocha containing milk and sugar. We're talking about black coffee and tea here. And embrace water as your beverage of choice before, during, and after workouts.

134. Drink Kombucha

Since the Chinese Tsin Dynasty in 221 B.C., kombucha tea has been used as a health elixir. Fans claim that it is packed with organic acids that build healthy tissues and normalize blood alkalinity, probiotics that benefit your digestive system, and live enzymes that help fuel the body's cells. It combats free radicals and has been used as a remedy for arthritis, constipation, obesity, arteriosclerosis, impotence, kidney stones, rheumatism, gout, and cancer. You can find kombucha at most health food stores.

If you choose to try kombucha, be sure to limit your intake to 4 ounces daily. If you have pre-existing health problems or drink excessive amounts of the tea, health problems may arise.

135. Drink Maté Tea

Maté tea is an herbal tea native to South America that is perfect for a midday energy boost. Maté tea has many of the same metabolism-boosting properties of coffee, but contains less caffeine so it won't make you nervous or jittery. Instead, you'll feel healthy, energetic, and ready to face the rest of your day.

However, be sure to drink maté tea in moderation only because, according to the Mayo Clinic, some studies indicate that prolonged use of maté tea may increase the risk of various types of cancer, including cancer of the mouth, esophagus, and lungs. Smoking in combination with maté tea seems to greatly increase the cancer risk.

136. Know How Many Calories You're Drinking

Beverages can add lots of calories, and you may not realize how many you're actually drinking. Being aware of the number of calories found in common beverages can help you make healthy choices and keep your metabolism running at full speed. Here's a list of drinks that may wake you up to the amount of calories you're taking in from beverages alone. All drinks are labeled for 8-ounce servings unless otherwise noted. Rather than listing all alcoholic beverages separately, please note that most mixed drinks range from 400 to 600 calories for 8 ounces, while dessert liquors can jump up to the 800–900 range. Most sodas are around 100 calories for 8 ounces, but most cans contain 12 ounces, or 150 calories.

Beverage	Calories	Beverage	Calories
Apple juice	95	Milk, 1%	102
Beer (Budweiser)	98	Milk, 2%	113
Beer (Bud Light)	72	Milk, whole	145
Club soda	0	Milkshake, chocolate	270
Coffee, black	2	Orange juice, freshly squeezed	102

Beverage	Calories	Beverage	Calories
Coffee, with cream	48	Prune juice	161
Coffee, with cream and sugar	91	Red Bull	100
Cranberry–apple juice drink	152	Red Bull, sugar-free	10
Diet soda	0	Tea, sweetened	77
Grape juice	138	Tea, unsweetened	2
Grapefruit juice, canned and sweetened	104	Tomato juice	39
Grapefruit juice, freshly squeezed	88	Tonic water	77
Hot cocoa	197	Wine, dessert	311
Lemonade	100	Wine, red	163
Milk, skim	79	Wine, white	154

137. Drink Out of Tall Glasses

We all know that our eyes can trick our minds, so be sure to pour your beverages into tall glasses (and fill them up with ice cubes for an extra metabolism boost) to make it look as though you're drinking more than you are. Don't fill glasses to the rim, and you'll be more likely to view the consumption as a treat rather than a chore. Also, invest in attractive glasses that you love, and even ice-cube trays in fancy shapes. Buy fresh lemon to perch on the edge of water glasses—the citrus will help kick your metabolism up a notch as well. Do whatever it takes to make drinking healthy, zero- or low-calorie beverages a lot more fun.

CHAPTER 9
Boost Your Metabolism by . . .
SNACKING SMARTLY

Include Snacks in Your Diet

Choose Healthy Snacks

Try Hummus

Have a Little Peanut Butter

Keep Healthy Snacks in Plain View

Take Healthy Snacks on the Road

Choose Fiber Snacks While Watching TV

Munch on Air-Popped Popcorn

Just Say No to Sugary Snacks

Eat Nutrient-Rich Fruits

Try Frozen Grapes

Make a Mango Smoothie

Make Snacks Part of Your Eating Plan for the Day

Eat Smaller Portion Snacks, Not Meal-Size Ones

Graze Throughout the Day

Hit the Pause Button

Don't Eat Before Going to Bed

138. Include Snacks in Your Diet

Contrary to popular belief, snacking—done right—can give your metabolism a boost! Here's why: When you slash too many calories from your diet, your body gets the signal that it should protect its reserves of carbs and fat, and your metabolism slows as a result. To prevent this, eat several small, low-fat, high-fiber snacks between meals to keep your body from going into "preservation" mode. Snacking in this manner will add to your total intake of essential nutrients for the day—that's always a good thing! You'll find that snacking will also take the edge off hunger between meals, so when you sit down to eat, you're more likely to consume fewer calories.

139. Choose Healthy Snacks

Try some of these smart snacks as part of your healthy eating plan:

- Half a bagel with peanut butter
- Raw vegetables with low-fat or fat-free dressing
- Fruit yogurt topped with low-fat granola cereal
- Low-fat cottage cheese topped with fresh fruit
- Fresh fruit
- Light microwave popcorn
- Pita bread stuffed with fresh veggies and low-fat dressing
- Low-fat string cheese
- Whole-grain cereal and fat-free milk
- Vegetable juice

140. Try Hummus

It's hard to complain about hummus. All of the ingredients used to produce it—chickpeas, olive or canola oil, pureed sesame seeds (also known as tahini), lemon juice, spices, and garlic—are extremely good for you and most are known to boost the metabolism. Chickpeas are an excellent source for energy; they're made of complex carbohydrates and protein, and tahini is rich in minerals, fatty acids, and amino acids. So, enjoy, but keep your intake in check because hummus is high in calories; if you're using it as a dip, it's easy to eat a lot of it. We recommend spreading 2 tablespoons of hummus on a slice of whole-grain bread or eating a ¼ cup of hummus with carrots or broccoli.

141. Have a Little Peanut Butter

Peanuts are a great source of energy. They contain 25 grams of protein per 100-gram serving, and most of the fat is mono- and polyunsaturated fat. They also are packed with niacin, which is one of the most effective vitamins for increasing your good cholesterol. Peanuts also have the flavonoid resveratrol—also found in red wine—that may contribute to fat loss. But, as we also know, peanuts and peanut butter are high in calories, so consume them in moderation.

142. Keep Healthy Snacks in Plain View

Store healthy snacks in attractive glass containers to keep them visible and easily accessible. Store fresh fruit in bowls on the counter and raw vegetables in plastic containers on the top shelf of your refrigerator. If you have unhealthy snacks, push them back in dark corners of cupboards you rarely use—or better yet, don't buy them in the first place. Train yourself to reach for the healthy snacks, make them easy to grab, and you'll soon become so accustomed to this behavior that it will be a natural habit.

143. Take Healthy Snacks on the Road

When traveling, to avoid having your hunger dictate your food choices, plan ahead to ensure you have healthy snacks on hand. Fruit, nut, and seed mixtures or slices of cheese with whole-wheat crackers, whole fruits, raw vegetables, or even low-sugar granola bars, are far preferable to chips, candy bars, milkshakes, or the myriad of poor choices that are readily available at every gas station or market. Also, take along bottles of water or fruit juice to quench your thirst.

144. Choose Fiber Snacks While Watching TV

Beyond the fact that you're totally sedentary while watching TV, this activity tends to be damaging to health because of mindless snacking. Try to avoid all buttery and salty options. Instead, choose low-calorie, high-fiber snacks such as carrots, berries, broccoli, celery, and apple slices. Even better? Turn off the television and take a walk, go for a jog, or spend some time working outdoors to burn calories and increase your metabolism.

145. Munch on Air-Popped Popcorn

Popcorn can be very fattening when you buy it at the movies, or when you buy the packaged microwave brands. Air-popped popcorn, however, is light and healthy and provides a high amount of fiber. Remember, anything that's difficult for your body to digest is a major metabolism booster! Get yourself an inexpensive air-popper and pop your own, adding just a dash of seasoning and light sprays of cholesterol-reducing oils. Steer clear of popping popcorn in oil or coating it in oils or butter, and you can enjoy popcorn as a nutritious snack.

146. Just Say No to Sugary Snacks

Because the hours between dinner and lunch can create a mini-fast, many crave sweets in the late afternoon. Before you reach for a candy bar, a piece of chocolate, or a brownie, seek out snacks that contain all three macronutrients—like carbohydrates, protein, and fat. Eating a low-fat piece of cheese with a few whole-wheat crackers, a cup of yogurt with strawberries or a few tablespoons of granola, or a healthy granola bar will satisfy your craving and keep your blood sugar and metabolism from crashing. Stay within the 150–200 calories range, and you'll not only be staving off a hunger that will cause you to overeat at dinner, you'll be priming your metabolic engine and avoiding hundreds of empty calories.

147. Eat Nutrient-Rich Fruits

Fruit's sweet flavor comes from fructose, a naturally occurring sugar that serves as a good source of energy. Fruit is full of healthy substances such as vitamin C, vitamin A, potassium, folic acid, antioxidants, phytochemicals, and fiber, just to name a few. Citrus fruits, berries, and melons are excellent sources of vitamin C. Dried fruits are available all year long and are an excellent source of many nutrients including fiber. Almost all fruits and vegetables are good for you, but some are better than others. When it comes to fruit, apples, bananas, berries, citrus fruit, and melons are your best bets because of their high fiber and nutrient content. Researchers at Scripps Clinic found that fruit eaters ate fewer calories overall compared to those not adding fruit to their diet. Fruit can help you satisfy sugar cravings, feel full longer, and eat less.

148. Try Frozen Grapes

If you're craving a sweet treat but don't want to blow your healthy eating habits, throw some grapes in the freezer and munch on them a few hours later when they're frosty. They taste like sorbet and they contain manganese, flavonoids, and B6—an excellent metabolism booster—which may lower your risk for heart disease. So you're getting a treat that's both healthy and sweet!

149. Make a Mango Smoothie

Mangos are packed with vitamins, minerals, and antioxidants. They are especially high in many carotenoids, including beta-carotene, and also come loaded with magnesium, potassium, phosphorous, selenium, folic acid, zinc, and A, B, and E vitamins. And, on top of all that, they contain an enzyme that has stomach-soothing properties and helps with digestion. Add some whey protein and water or low-fat yogurt to thicken up your drink and you've got a super-healthy, immune-boosting, metabolism-blasting snack!

150. Make Snacks Part of Your Eating Plan for the Day

Eating daily snacks is a great way to make sure your metabolism is at its peak. Don't grab a handful of chips or a candy bar but munch on healthy foods that provide important nutrients throughout the day. You'll supply your body with energy and make it do a little work in the digestive process. Here's how to snack smartly:

- **Choose whole-grain products**: Whole grains are rich in fiber and complex carbohydrates, so they boost your metabolism for longer periods because they require more effort to digest.
- **Have a fruit or vegetable**: Fruits and vegetables are filled with vitamins, minerals, and fiber. They will fill you up without adding many calories to your diet, and some may even cause your body to go into a calorie deficit in the process!
- **Nibble on a handful of nuts or seeds**: Nuts and seeds provide protein and monounsaturated fat, so they will help you feel full longer. Just don't eat more than a small handful because they're also high in calories.
- **Try low-fat dairy products**: Cheese, yogurt, and other dairy products are good sources of calcium, protein, and many other vitamins and minerals, but read the labels to make sure you're not eating added sugars.

151. Eat Smaller Portion Snacks, Not Meal-Size Ones

Snacking is not meant to be an extra meal. A healthy snack should be portion sensitive—a small amount of something nutritious—to keep the metabolic fires burning and tide you over to your next meal. Snacks

BOOST YOUR METABOLISM BY . . . **SNACKING SMARTLY**

should be small amounts of nutrient-dense foods ideally consisting of protein and carbohydrate. A few whole-wheat crackers with a wedge of farmer's cheese; ¼ cup of cottage cheese with half an orange; a hard-boiled egg and half an apple; a slice of whole-wheat toast with thinly spread peanut butter, and so on—just enough to provide a steady source of energy throughout the day or to stave off hunger that would cause you to overeat at your next meal.

152. Graze Throughout the Day

Rather than downing two or three super-size meals a day, which actually trains your metabolism to slow down, eat smaller meals more frequently. Researchers have long confirmed that eating small (healthy) meals or snacks every three to four hours works well to keep your metabolism burning and churning. If you make your snacks and meals healthy, you'll likely reduce your caloric intake at regular meals, and lose weight over the long haul. Make sure, however, that you are not choosing high-fat, high-calorie carbohydrates, such as chips or cookies.

153. Hit the Pause Button

When snacking, take a break. You know how it goes: You're shoveling in small morsels of food and lose count of how much you've eaten, until suddenly you realize you ate way more than you intended to eat. Try taking a break between bites; take a physical pause and distract yourself by focusing your attention on something else. Call a friend, load the dishwasher, look for the CD you misplaced upstairs, dust the television, or do whatever it takes to stop unconsciously shoveling food into your mouth. Often, you'll find that taking a break will help you realize that you're no longer hungry and give you the respite you need to make a better choice.

154. Don't Eat Before Going to Bed

Contrary to the popular idea that you shouldn't eat after 7 P.M., the amount of calories you consume throughout the day is actually more important than when you eat them. However, it is best to eat more calories earlier in the day and make sure the last meal of the day is light on calories and fat. You can eat after 7 P.M., but keep that snack or small meal closer to 200–300 calories, and eat it at least two hours before bedtime. If you're convinced that you need something just before bed, limit it to 100 calories and try to eat at least 30 minutes before lying down. It's easier for your stomach to digest food while you're still awake and sitting.

BOOST YOUR METABOLISM BY . . . **SNACKING SMARTLY**

CHAPTER 10
Boost Your Metabolism by . . .
KEEPING UP THAT CALCIUM

Consume Calcium

Choose Foods Rich in Calcium

Try Dairy

Drink Milk

Eat Yogurt

Eat Reduced-Fat Cheese

Eat Broccoli Sprouts

Eat Spinach and Other Dark Leafy Greens

Eat Kale and Other Brassica Vegetables

Eat Fish with Edible Bones

Try Sardines

155. Consume Calcium

Calcium is an important part of a balanced diet. That's because calcium is not only important for strengthening bones (which is especially important because it helps prevent musculoskeletal injuries during exercise), it also regulates your blood pressure, helps secrete hormones and digestive enzymes, assists directly with weight loss, regulates heart muscle function, and helps boost your metabolism. One animal study even showed an increase in core temperature related to calcium consumption. Remember, when body heat rises, so does metabolic rate. Not a dairy fan? Don't worry; many foods are rich in calcium.

156. Choose Foods Rich in Calcium

The easiest way to stock up on your calcium needs is by eating dairy products like milk, cheese, and yogurt. But there are many other foods that are also rich in calcium. They include dark green leafy vegetables like broccoli, spinach, kale, and collards; fish with edible bones; calcium-fortified soy milk; tofu made with calcium; shelled almonds; turnips; mustard greens; sesame seeds; blackstrap molasses; calcium-fortified cereals; and calcium-fortified orange juice.

157. Try Dairy

Dairy products help boost metabolism and build strong bones because of their high calcium levels. Some studies have even suggested that the calcium in dairy products may facilitate weight loss.

One such study featured three groups of obese subjects, each of whom was on a diet that would promote a weight loss of a pound a

BOOST YOUR METABOLISM BY . . . **KEEPING UP THAT CALCIUM**

week for 24 weeks. Each group received a different amount of calcium: The lowest received 430 mg/day through their diet; the middle group received 770 mg/day through the same diet, plus supplements; and the third group received 1,100 mg/day wholly through diet. At the end of the study, the group receiving the lowest calcium had lost nearly 15 pounds, the middle group had lost 19 pounds, and the group that ate the most calcium-rich foods had lost 24 pounds, 66 percent of which was fat from their abdominal area (as opposed to the low-calcium group which lost 19 percent of fat from their abdominal area). As you can see, it pays to include dairy in your diet.

158. Drink Milk

A serving of milk, especially cow's milk, helps build strong bones by supplying the body with nearly 30 percent of its daily calcium needs and 20 percent of its phosphorus needs, as well as plenty of vitamins A, D, and K, and two of the B vitamins that are needed for heart health and energy production. If you're lactose intolerant or are opposed to drinking cow's milk but still want the milk you drink to have a positive impact on your metabolism, make sure your rice, soy, or almond milk is fortified with these vitamins and minerals.

159. Eat Yogurt

Yogurt is an excellent source of calcium that also provides about 9 grams of animal protein per 6-ounce serving plus vitamin B2, vitamin B12, potassium, and magnesium. One of the most beneficial aspects of yogurt comes from the use of active, good bacteria known as probiotics.

Probiotics adjust the natural balance of organisms, known as microflora, in the intestines to aid digestion. To make sure your favorite brand of yogurt contains active cultures, look for labeling that says "live and active cultures," or for words such as *Bifidus regularis*, *L. bulgaricus*, *S. thermophilus*, or *bifidobacterium*.

160. Eat Reduced-Fat Cheese

Cheese is a great source for protein, vitamins, and minerals, but it is also high in calories and saturated fat. So, while you shouldn't cut it out altogether, it would be wise to make a habit of choosing reduced-fat cheese, which has about 30 to 40 percent fewer calories and less fat. Try the following suggestions so you don't overdo how much fat you're eating:

- Use half of what you would normally use in recipes.
- To boost flavor but reduce calories, use higher-flavor cheeses sparingly: Parmesan, Romano, blue cheese, Gorgonzola, goat, feta, or extra-sharp Cheddar.
- Eat cheese with lower fat alongside higher-fiber foods, such as apples, pears, whole-grain bread or crackers, or beans so you feel full faster.

161. Eat Broccoli Sprouts

Broccoli sprouts boost enzymes in the body, while detoxifying potential carcinogens. Researchers estimate that broccoli sprouts provide 10 to 100 times the power of mature broccoli to neutralize carcinogens. Dr. Paul Talalay, researcher at the Johns Hopkins School of Medicine, found that three-day-old broccoli sprouts consistently contained 20 to 50 times the amount of chemo-protective compounds found in mature broccoli heads, offering a simple, dietary means of chemically reducing cancer risk. The antioxidants found in broccoli sprouts may help boost metabolism as well as prevent several types of cancer, heart disease, macular degeneration, and stomach ulcers. They may also help reduce cholesterol levels.

162. Eat Spinach and Other Dark Leafy Greens

Popeye wasn't playing around. Spinach is one of the best foods you can possibly eat. Loaded with calcium, folic acid, vitamin K, iron, vitamin C, fiber, carotenoids, lutein, and bioflavonoids, spinach is low in calories and it is a nutritional powerhouse. Other dark leafy greens like collards, Swiss chard, turnip greens, and bok choy are also excellent sources of calcium. Try adding spinach and other dark leafy greens to salads or soups, omelets or quiche, or as a replacement for iceberg or romaine lettuce on sandwiches.

163. Eat Kale and Other Brassica Vegetables

Loaded with cancer-fighting antioxidants and rich in calcium, kale is one of the healthiest foods in the vegetable kingdom; together with its cousin, broccoli, kale offers strong protection against cancer and other diseases. Kale and other vegetables in the Brassica family contain a potent glucosinolate phytonutrient that actually boosts your body's detoxification enzymes, clearing potentially carcinogenic substances more quickly from your body. More common members of the prestigious

Brassica family of vegetables include cabbage, broccoli, Brussels sprouts, cauliflower, collards, mustard greens, bok choy, and broccoli rabe or rapini. With so many choices, take advantage of having at least one each day of the week.

164. Eat Fish with Edible Bones

When you dine on fish, you're eating a complete protein; that is, you're getting all of the amino acids your body requires for proper nutrition. They're also good sources for many of the B vitamins, and fattier fishes are good for getting your A and D vitamins. But if you want an extra helping of calcium to help maintain your skeleton, munch on fish with small, soft, edible bones such as canned anchovies, sardines, chum salmon, or jack mackerel.

165. Try Sardines

Sardines are packed with nutrients, including calcium, coenzyme Q10, protein, and potassium. They are particularly good sources of calcium, providing the same amount of calcium as a glass of whole milk—plus balanced amounts of vitamin D and phosphorus, needed for the effective absorption of calcium.

CHAPTER 11
Boost Your Metabolism by . . .
WATCHING YOUR WEIGHT

Know When You Need to Trim Down

Research Diets

Jettison Bad Habits

Keep a Food Diary for One Week

Set Realistic Goals

Whittle Your Waist

Don't Crash-Diet

Lose 10 Percent of Your Excess
Body Weight

Eat More Fruits and Vegetables

Eat to Live, Don't Live to Eat

Distinguish Between Hunger
and Cravings

Chew Gum

Follow the 90/10 Rule

Create and Adhere to Restaurant Rules

Use Visualization

166. Know When You Need to Trim Down

You already know that a healthy body equals a healthy metabolism, but part of having a healthy body means maintaining or reaching a healthy weight. Ideal weights are typically based on your gender and your height, but there can be wide variance in what is most healthful and most desirable. In general, it's better to gauge the percentage of fat, or body mass index (BMI), that you are carrying. For a man, a body fat percentage of 18 percent to 25 percent is not bad if he's over forty. For women over forty, 22 percent to 27 percent is not bad.

You can also gauge your need to reduce the amount of calories you are consuming. If you are a woman who exercises moderately, your daily caloric intake should not exceed 1,500 to 1,600 calories a day; if you are a man who exercises moderately, your caloric intake should not exceed 1,800 to 2,000 calories per day. These calories should come from a balanced diet that includes lean protein, good fats, and nutrient-rich carbohydrates.

167. Research Diets

If you are considering a diet plan, see your doctor first. Ask him or her to recommend the best long-term plan for you, and if there are any drawbacks to whatever diet you are considering. You can also access a lot of in-depth information, including expert opinions, on *www.webmd.com/diet/evaluate-latest-diets*. This site has information on everything from fad diets to medically supervised diets. Study the facts before you leap into a weight-loss plan, and make the right choice for your body—and your metabolism!

168. Jettison Bad Habits

If you smoke, quit. If you drink too much, stop or at least drink in moderation. If you aren't getting enough exercise, join a gym. If the only fruits and veggies in your kitchen are made of wax, make a concerted effort to add more fresh items to your daily diet. If you eat ice cream every day, cut back to once a week. If you only eat white bread, switch to whole grain. If you never eat breakfast, eat a healthy breakfast every day. If you can't remember the last time you saw a doctor, make an appointment for a checkup. In short, do what you must to make your lifestyle more healthful in every way. Remember, the healthier you are, the better your metabolism will be.

169. Keep a Food Diary for One Week

Studies show most people dramatically underestimate their caloric consumption each day. To investigate the truth, keep a detailed food diary for one whole week. Write down every single bite you eat, what sauce you use, and what beverages you drink. If you suck on a mint, write it down. Once you have the data, you'll see where you can cut down or substitute healthier choices. This will bolster your consciousness and help you improve your overall eating habits.

170. Set Realistic Goals

Losing a dramatic amount of weight or completely upgrading your physique can seem like a daunting task. You basically set yourself up to fail if you vow to lose 10 pounds in two weeks or 25 pounds in two months. That's why it's vital to set short-, middle-, and long-range goals. For example, say, "Today I will avoid starchy carbs after three o'clock," "I will lose two pounds by next week," or "I will drop seven percent of my body fat in six months." These are goals you can reach—and you'll be healthier, more fit, and feeling good about yourself.

171. Whittle Your Waist

Men with waistline circumferences over 40 inches and women with waists greater than 35 inches have a significantly greater risk of a heart attack than their slimmer pals. Use this knowledge to create a nutritious, metabolism-boosting diet. Follow it with vigor and determination, and you'll not only whittle your waist, you'll whittle your hips, thighs, arms, and everything else!

172. Don't Crash-Diet

Any dietary plan that asks you to severely limit calories (less than 1,000 calories a day) actually thwarts your desire to boost your metabolism. It will effectively shut down your metabolism. First, your body believes it's starving and will fight to conserve fat. Second, such a restrictive diet may lack vital nutrients that play an important role in boosting metabolism and helping your body function better overall. Third, rapid weight loss may look or feel good, but it's likely to erode muscle mass—and muscles burn fat. The more muscles you have, the higher your rate of metabolism. Finally, study after study after study has shown that most radical diets lead to a return to previous eating habits and a return of all the fat the dieter shed, plus more. Changing your eating habits and eating a balanced, healthy diet is the only truly effective way to lose fat and boost your metabolism.

173. Lose 10 Percent of Your Excess Body Weight

We're sure you have your reasons for wanting to rev up your metabolism or lose weight. But, one of them should be health. Did you know that by losing just 5 to 10 percent of your excess body weight, you can lower your blood pressure, cholesterol, insulin, and triglyceride levels? Losing weight shouldn't be just about looking good. It should also be about staying healthy.

174. Eat More Fruits and Vegetables

Some foods are better for you than others. The key is to eat a diverse diet, with an emphasis on those foods that pack the heaviest nutritional punch. Fruits and vegetables are an important part of any health regimen because they are loaded with essential nutrients in their most natural and useful form—and the more fruits and vegetables you eat the more satiated you will feel and you will be able to *avoid* high-calorie foods and fat. The majority of Americans don't consume nearly enough fruits and vegetables. Government health officials suggest a minimum of five servings of fruit and vegetables daily—twice the amount suggested for meat and dairy.

175. Eat to Live, Don't Live to Eat

Food can be incredibly enjoyable—and addictive—but its main purpose is to keep you alive and kicking. If you want to live a long and healthy life, you need to eat foods that truly nourish your body. Plus, if you are putting in extra efforts to burn calories and lose or maintain your weight, why would you wipe out all that effort by consuming empty calories? Rather than eating whatever is in front you, focus on food choices that will nourish your body and keep your metabolic engine running at peak efficiency. To think thin and live thin, make an effort to schedule fun activities that don't revolve around food. Instead of dinner plans, make plans to play sports, go dancing, or see a show.

176. Distinguish Between Hunger and Cravings

One important step in making sure you don't overeat is to challenge yourself when you think you're hungry. Are you hungry or are you having an emotional craving for food? One way of determining the difference is by having a glass of water. Often when you think you're hungry, you're actually thirsty. If the feeling doesn't diminish or if you're experiencing more serious signals such as headache, lack of concentration, or physical hunger pains, head to the kitchen and make a healthy snack.

177. Chew Gum

Gum chewing can help boost your metabolism in a couple of ways. First, if you're having trouble with overeating, just the simple act of chewing gum can help you hold off on grabbing foods that aren't metabolism boosting throughout the day. Second, a Mayo Clinic study concluded that gum chewing actually boosted metabolism by up to 20 percent and could help participants lose up to 10 pounds a year! That's a lot of Double Bubble!

178. Follow the 90/10 Rule

People who focus on overall fitness know that eating healthy is not an all-or-nothing activity. They know that if they make the majority of their food choices great, they can indulge occasionally. Create a 90/10 rule of your own: If 90 percent of your meals are full of lean protein, produce, lean dairy, and whole grains, indulging in less-than-nutritious choices 10 percent of the time won't slow down your metabolism.

179. Create and Adhere to Restaurant Rules

Eating in restaurants often leads to a downfall. Because it's so tempting to let down your guard and eat all the things you'd normally limit when you're eating out, set some ground rules to minimize caloric or fat overload. For example, never order meat that has been fried or sautéed; always request that it be cooked without oil or butter. Do the same for your veggies, although it's great to eat them raw. Keep baskets of bread off the table; you don't need that! Request all sauces and dressings on the side, and drizzle very small amounts on the dish. Stick with water for your beverage or the occasional glass of red wine. Make it a golden rule never to order dessert for one, and when sharing, take three small bites and put down your fork or spoon. End your meal with coffee or tea for a treat.

180. Use Visualization

Imagination is a wonderful thing—it allows us to visualize ourselves stronger, thinner, healthier, or whatever we desire. Many believe that visualization leads to manifestation, particularly if you practice daily. When you wake up, spend 5 to 10 minutes visualizing yourself as leaner and sexier: the picture of health. If you have trouble visualizing yourself that way, find a picture of someone in a magazine who has the body you desire, paste your head on it, and place it on your bathroom mirror or the refrigerator. What you focus on is what you manifest, so focus on being the healthiest you that you can be. Go for it!

CHAPTER 12

Boost Your Metabolism by . . .

MOVING YOUR BODY

181. Understand Your Body's Need for Exercise

Regular physical activity helps keep your muscles toned and strong, maintains bone strength and density, and improves and maintains your heart and lung functions. Exercise also builds stamina, improves flexibility, boosts your immune system, makes sex more fun, reduces your risk of cancer, improves your reflexes, lowers stress, and benefits your overall physical and mental health. But even more important, exercise is a great way to ensure your metabolism functions at maximum capacity.

Exercise can be divided into three specific types: general activity, activities to build stamina, and exercises to increase strength and flexibility. If you want to age well, maximize your metabolism, and add many more active and vibrant years to your life, it's important to incorporate all three aspects of exercise into your lifestyle. It's also highly important that you begin slowly, set realistic goals, and see a doctor before you begin any new regimen. Don't overdo it, but remember that the harder you're working, the harder your metabolism is working, too!

182. Understand the Importance of Heart Rates

When you know your resting heart rate, you can make sure you're reaching your full potential when you exercise. That's because your pulse, measured in beats per minute, tells you how much effort your heart and body are putting in. The American College of Sports Medicine (ACSM) recommends that you exercise at aerobic intensity levels of 60 to 90 percent of your maximum heart rate. But, if you're new to exercise, we recommend exercising so that your heart rate is 60 percent or less of its maximum potential and progressing gradually into higher levels of intensity so you don't put too much strain on the heart muscle.

While it may seem that you are only putting in a light effort, you are still benefiting your metabolism by training your cardiovascular system to work more efficiently and by burning calories.

183. Determine Your Heart-Rate Zone

To estimate what your heart rate or pulse should be when you exercise, use this formula:

Subtract your age from 220. For example: If you are forty years old, then the answer is 180. This number is your estimated maximum heart rate in beats per minute.

Now, multiply that number (e.g., 180) by .65 and .85. The two numbers (117 and 153) tell you the range in which your heart rate should be during exercise.

You should spend the majority of your exercise time with your heart rate in the lower part of the range, reaching the higher part of the range only during brief interval sessions. If you're very fit, you can use a slightly different formula to determine the range of your heart rate during exercise. As a first step, subtract your age from 205, and then do the rest of the calculations described.

184. Monitor Your Heart Rate When You Exercise

When you're exercising, it's important to keep track of your heart rate so that you can make sure you're working out in a range that is maximizing your calorie-burning potential. If you're not working out on a machine that keeps track of your rate, you can either use a heart rate monitor or two of your fingers.

If you're measuring manually, place two fingers gently just below the top of the jaw on the side of your neck over your carotid artery or over the radial artery located just where your wrist bends. Count for 15 seconds, then multiply the number of beats you felt by 4 to estimate your beats per minute (bpm). If you're doing this when you're at rest, this number represents your approximate resting heart rate.

If you prefer to have a monitor keep track of your heart rate—which is, admittedly, easier when you're in the middle of a workout—find a heart monitor that includes a strap that goes around your chest and a watch-like device that will allow you to easily read the results.

185. Burn Those Calories

Your body is working all the time: pumping blood, processing food, even thinking. The body's unit of measurement for the amount of work it's doing is the calorie. When you sit and think, you burn about a calorie per minute. When you take a walk, your body might burn from 3 to 6 calories a minute. For every liter of oxygen (per kilogram of body weight) you process during aerobic exercise, the body burns 5 calories. The more energy you use, the more oxygen you process, and the more calories you burn. Ideally, you should burn 300 calories or more per exercise session.

Your body's calorie usage during any given activity is determined by your weight, your fitness level, and the amount of work you're doing. Because of the difference in the muscle/fat ratio of their bodies, as well as their fitness levels, a slight, older woman burns fewer calories taking a walk than a young, muscular man.

186. Feel Free to Fidget

You probably know a few fidgety people. These people's bodies simply tell them to move more. They're always busy, always moving, and rarely sit still. They tap their feet, drum their fingers on the table, and are constantly on the go! It sounds silly, but fidgeting can actually burn between 500 and 1,000 calories per day, about 1 pound per week! So go ahead. Feel free to fidget and watch your metabolic furnace burn up those calories!

187. Exercise Six to Eight Hours a Week

With 168 hours in each week, it really isn't irrational to suggest that you engage in 6 to 8 hours of deliberate exercise per week. Because of the time spent sleeping, eating, driving, watching television, and sitting at a desk working, most people lead fairly sedentary lives. Exercise vigorously most days of the week and you'll be more likely to achieve your physical goals. Exercise, by the way, should require you to huff, puff, grunt, and wince. Challenging yourself is how you make progress. If you set aside deliberate time for legitimate exercise and work hard, your body—and your metabolic rate—will respond accordingly.

188. Love Your Muscles

The human body is an amazing machine, and muscles are a large part of what drives it. There are about 650 muscles in the body, and they provide all kinds of support and propulsion. The skeletal muscles, in conjunction with tendons and ligaments, support the body's frame and give it shape; smooth muscles line body organs; and cardiac muscles pump the heart. Muscles are at work constantly to adjust your posture, move your body parts, keep you upright, operate certain bodily functions, and generate heat in your body.

Skeletal muscles work in pairs so that when you move, one contracts and another relaxes. This way, all the parts that need to bend can also return to their normal position. Muscles need the nutrients and oxygen transported by your blood to keep them functioning; the better your muscles are cared for, the better they perform. And the better they perform—on a regular basis—the more you boost your metabolism.

189. Protect Your Muscles

Done properly, exercise strengthens muscles, helping them to do their job better. If you overwork a muscle group (even without intending to), you can strain and even tear your muscles, which can force you to stop exercising until the muscles heal. To avoid this, treat your muscles with respect. Warm them up, don't push them too hard, and help strengthen them properly by stretching carefully and thoroughly.

190. Strive to Become a Long, Lean, Metabolism-Boosting Machine

Exercise keeps our bodies and all of their parts working efficiently. When your heart is fit, it beats more strongly but uses less energy to keep pumping. When your muscles are fit, they can lift more and work longer without feeling stress or getting hurt. When your entire body is fit, you burn more calories, sleep better at night, and have a stronger immune system and higher metabolic rate. When you exercise regularly and effectively, your body is lean, sleek, and capable. You'll need to do 30 minutes of moderate activity daily (which can be broken up into 10-minute sessions) to stay healthy, and three or four high-intensity workouts each week to stay truly fit. The more you exercise, the more calories you burn, and the stronger your heart and muscles are.

191. Up the Amount of General Exercise You Get Daily

General exercise includes any activity that requires the use of muscles, such as walking around the block, doing housework or yard work, and taking the stairs rather than the elevator. A 30-minute walk can make a significant difference, as will any other activities that involve total body movement—and we don't mean moving your thumb while playing video games or moving your arms while knitting. Move your body to boost your metabolism and to vastly improve your overall health.

192. Increase Your Stamina

Exercises that increase stamina greatly benefit the heart and lungs. These activities require far more exertion than general physical activity and include running, cycling, swimming laps, playing tennis, dancing, in-line skating, and playing handball or racquetball. The goal is to strengthen the heart and lungs by working both at full capacity. If you haven't exercised in a while, it's a good idea to start slowly and gradually increase the amount of exercise you do in a week. As your stamina increases, you'll find it easier to do more and more. If you're over forty, it's also wise to get a physical exam from your doctor before starting any type of stamina-building exercise—just to be on the safe side.

193. Improve Your Strength and Flexibility

Exercises to increase strength and flexibility include weightlifting (whether through the use of free weights or the kind of weight machines found in most gyms) and yoga, Pilates, and similar stretching activities. Maintaining strength, muscle tone, and flexibility is especially important during our middle and senior years, and there are additional benefits as well, such as improving bone density and reducing risk of injury from accidents. Weight-bearing exercises are particularly important for women because they can help prevent the onset of osteoporosis later in life by maintaining bone density before, during, and after menopause. And you don't have to lift weights until you bulge like Mr. Universe; most health specialists say 30 to 40 minutes of weight training a week is sufficient to maintain optimum health.

Strength-training exercises isolate muscles and muscle groups and build muscular strength and endurance. Improvements in muscular strength cause the body to burn more calories, even at rest. These exercises include weight training, calisthenics, and sometimes activities like yoga or ballet. You stimulate muscle growth by pushing your muscles a bit beyond what they are accustomed to. To strengthen muscles, they must experience resistance, or an opposing force. The terms *resistance training* and *strength training* are used interchangeably and simply mean the process (just described) used to produce strength; the term *weight training* refers to using weight or weights as a form of resistance that produces gains in strength.

194. Choose the Right Exercise

No single physical activity or exercise approach is right for all populations; the needs and abilities of men are different from those of women, just as the needs and abilities of younger people are different from those in their senior years. The goals of regular exercise are also as varied as the individuals who engage in it. Some people exercise to lose weight; others want to increase muscle mass, strength, or endurance. Whatever your personal goal may be, the key to success is perseverance. It may take some trial and error before you find the most satisfying and effective exercise regimen for your individual needs and abilities, but the time spent is well worth it. As any doctor will tell you, exercise is one of the key components to adding many more healthful years to your life.

195. Seek Variety

The fittest bodies and healthiest people get that way due to a variety of types of exercises, such as walking, weightlifting, and yoga or bicycling, swimming, and gardening. The more variety in your exercise program, the more likely it is that your body will increase in strength, endurance, and flexibility—and the less likely it is that you'll suffer from overuse injuries.

A well-rounded exercise regimen should strengthen muscles, benefit the heart and lungs, and build endurance. For optimum results, alternate weight training, aerobics, and circuit training. Relying on only one form of exercise will not benefit your entire body. For example, weightlifting strengthens your muscles, but you'll also need some cardiovascular activity, such as aerobics, to benefit your heart and lungs.

EMPHASIZING AEROBIC EXERCISE

196. Understand the Benefits of Aerobic Exercise

Aerobic exercise is essential to boosting your metabolism. Whether you play tennis, swim, run, or work out on the elliptical machine, it's important to get at least 150 minutes of moderate-intensity exercise each week to keep your heart healthy and get in shape. Aerobic exercise causes your body to consume more oxygen as you breathe harder, and it trains the heart, blood vessels, and lungs to operate more efficiently, which, in turn, helps improve your metabolism.

To ensure that your aerobic exercise is effective, work a major muscle group, do it continuously for at least 20 minutes, and work harder than you would at rest. For example, turning a stroll into a fast walk, turning splashing in the pool into a five-lap race, or turning a neighborhood bike ride into a spinning class are all examples of regular activity becoming aerobic activity.

197. Choose Aerobic Exercise to Feel Great

Aerobic exercise does for the body what no other activity can because of a crucial process: the utilization of oxygen. You take in oxygen all the time just by breathing, of course. But when you participate in aerobic exercises, you take in greater amounts of oxygen, and it is delivered more deeply into the body because the heart, lungs, and muscles are working harder. Circulation increases, and with it, oxygen delivery. This is beneficial for your body and your metabolism, and it makes you feel great!

The body actually craves a higher aerobic level, and the workout actually improves the working of the body not only during exercise but also at rest. No other exercise makes us feel better.

198. Choose High-Octane Activities

If you want to lose weight, you need to select activities that will burn maximum calories. In general, light activities—cleaning your house, doing office work, or playing baseball or golf—burn 300 calories per hour for an average-size man and 240 for an average-size woman. Moderate activity—walking briskly, gardening, bicycling, dancing, or playing basketball—will burn 460 calories for men and 370 for women. Strenuous activity—jogging, playing football, or swimming—will burn 730 calories for men and 580 for women. Very strenuous activity—running, racquetball, or skiing—burns 920 calories for men and 740 for women.

Here is a chart that provides an idea of the variance in calories burned by activities. These calorie amounts are extremely approximate. Gender, age, ethnicity, muscle mass, and other individual characteristics have not been factored into these data. This chart is a way for you to clearly see the need for aerobic activities. For more accurate estimates, you can go to various websites and search for *calories burned while exercising*. Also, try *www.healthstatus.com/calculate/cbc*.

Activity	Estimated Calories Used
Bed rest, sleeping	60 per hour
Taking a shower	65 for 15 minutes
Eating a meal	70 per 30 minutes
Reading, watching TV	75 per hour
Sewing	80 per hour
Grocery shopping	90 per hour
Sexual intimacy	108 per hour
Brain work: computer, heavy concentrating	110 per hour

BOOST YOUR METABOLISM BY . . . **EMPHASIZING AEROBIC EXERCISE**

Activity	Estimated Calories Used
Playing fetch with your dog	115 per hour
Chasing after kids	120 per hour
Driving a vehicle	120 per hour
Busily cleaning house	130 per hour
Walking (moderate)	130 per hour
Horseback riding	130 per hour
Bicycling (6 mph)	135 per hour
Shopping at a mall	135 per hour
Bowling	145 per hour
Wrestling	180 for a 10–15 minute match
Heavy housework	230 per hour
Weeding a garden	230 per hour
Walking (2½ mph)	250 per hour
Playing golf/golf cart	250 per hour
Playing golf/carrying clubs	370 per hour
Softball, soccer, free-style swimming	260 per hour
Swimming	260 per hour
Skateboarding	275 per hour
Line dancing	280 per hour
Lawn mowing	295 per hour
Badminton, volleyball	340 per hour
Tennis, doubles	350 per hour
Martial arts	345 per hour
Water aerobics	360 per hour

Activity	Estimated Calories Used
Low-impact aerobic dance	385 per hour
Bicycling (12 mph)	385 per hour
Hiking, rock climbing, uphill	390 per hour
Dancing to rock and roll music	400 per hour
Competitive bowling	400 per hour
Step aerobics	400 per hour
Power walking (4½ mph)	400 per hour
Spinning class in a gym	440 per hour
High-impact aerobic dance	440 per hour
Football, hockey, basketball	460 per hour
Jump rope, continuous	480 per hour
Cross-country ski machine	500 per hour
Tennis, singles	510 per hour
Bicycling (12–14 mph)	530 per hour
Circuit weight training	540 per hour
Stair climbing in a gym	600 per hour
Jogging	600 per hour
Squash	650 per hour
Running (10 mph)	700 per hour
Athletic swimming	700 per hour
Cross-country skiing	700 per hour
Biking (14 mph)	700 per hour
Racquetball	700 per hour
Elliptical rider or rowing machine	850 per hour

BOOST YOUR METABOLISM BY . . . **EMPHASIZING AEROBIC EXERCISE**

199. Increase Your Workout Intensity

Moderate-intensity exercise gets your heart pumping, but not in an overly stressful, breathless way. This kind of exercise helps you develop endurance. High-intensity exercise is tough; you breathe heavily and are overloading your heart and muscles. You need a mixture of both kinds of intensity to stay fit. When you push your intensity levels, your body responds by becoming stronger and burning more calories.

To improve your fitness level, you need to work your body harder than it is used to working, which means you need to overload or increase the intensity and/or duration of your exercise regimen. Research has found that your body adapts to the stress of working harder by becoming stronger. For example, if you walk 2 miles five days a week, eventually walking those 2 miles will get easier, and you'll be able to work longer or faster or both. Your heart becomes stronger and more efficient using this overload principle, but you can also apply this principle to the other components of physical fitness, including muscle strength, muscle endurance, and flexibility.

By systematically overloading your muscles in both strength and endurance (lifting more weight or lifting weight for longer), as well as in flexibility (stretching further and more extensively), you will also be able to make gains in those fitness elements. Lifting weights and stretching in a regular strengthening program allows you to create a body that is more capable and fitter than it was before. The harder you exercise, the higher the levels of both fat and sugar that you'll burn. If you want to lose weight, burn off fat, and boost your metabolism, you'll need to gradually work your way up to more intense levels of exercise.

200. Increase Your RPM

Revolutions per minute (RPM) are measured as cadences on many cardio exercise machines. Typically, you have a choice of keeping your RPM low and increasing the resistance, which means you row or bike at a slower pace but face greater resistance, or increasing your RPM and lowering the resistance. Both are actually good for you, but if you want to burn more fat calories and keep your metabolic rate higher for a longer period, research has shown that high RPM with low-to-moderate resistance is more effective.

201. Play Tennis

Engaging in any court-based sport provides a good workout, but you only need one other person to start a game of tennis. It builds agility, hand-eye coordination, and works all the major muscle groups—and that helps your metabolism. Since the game is played in short bursts during which you're swinging your racquet or sprinting after a ball, it offers fat-burning benefits similar to those found in traditional interval training (see entry 233). A 150-pound individual can expect to burn more than 400 calories each hour and enjoy a competitive sport in the process.

202. Try Racquetball

One of the great things about this sport is that you'll burn a lot of calories even when you're starting out. A 150-pound person can expect to burn 500 calories at the beginning and push this into the 800s as he becomes more agile and gains stamina. In this interval-style sport that provides aerobic and anaerobic benefits, you'll run nearly 2 miles an hour and you won't even notice it—although your heart, waistline, and metabolism will!

203. Try Spinning Classes

Spinning on a stationary bike is a proven way to reduce body fat and expend calories, but it is much more than that. Spinning also helps you to strengthen joints, lower raised cholesterol, and increase energy levels. In terms of calories burned, about 10 minutes of spinning burns about 115 calories. If you took a spinning class every day over a year for at least 10 minutes a day, it could lead to a 12-pound weight loss. Spinning offers opportunities to strengthen your large leg muscles and increase your workout intensity by adding resistance and speed.

204. Try Cross-Country Skiing

During those winter months when running may not be an option, why not break out the cross-country skis? A 150-pound person can burn up to 900 calories per hour as she strengthens the muscles in her shoulders, back, chest, abdomen, buttocks, and legs using the kick and glide technique. If you're looking forward to starting a cross-country routine, we recommend preparing with exercises that work the upper- and lower-body muscle groups such as cycling, walking, swimming, and rowing.

205. Try Roller Skating

If you want to build strong legs, gain balance, and reduce your overall body fat while you get an aerobic workout, pick up a pair of roller skates or in-line skates. A 150-pound person will burn between 400 and 500 calories skating, so if he were to alternate his workouts between skating, cycling, and swimming, he'd burn a significant number of calories during the week and have fun doing it!

206. Join a Rowing Club

Rowing burns a lot of calories because it exercises larger muscle groups in both the upper and lower body. It is, in fact, one of the best forms of total body aerobic exercise because it involves all the major muscle groups. Also, within 10 minutes of rowing, your body gets into a rhythm that lights your metabolic fire. Rowing tones the arms and builds upper-body strength. Rowing for 25 minutes is aerobically equal to 40 minutes on a stationary bike. In a kayak or rowboat, you can get a workout targeting the core areas of your body, but if you like working out with others, join a rowing club.

Basically, rowing takes two forms. When rowers have an oar in each hand, it's called sculling. When rowers have both hands on one oar, it is called sweep rowing. Rowing is a low-impact exercise but does require a degree of agility, grace, and teamwork. Rowing as a team teaches you to work together for maximum effectiveness. The boat advances more rapidly when the team members row quickly and in unison. So make some new friends, learn the art of rowing, get in a regular workout, and feel good as your body becomes trim and toned—and your metabolism ratchets up.

207. Embrace Jumping Jacks

Good old-fashioned jumping jacks provide a great aerobic exercise that gets your heart pumping, carries oxygen to your lungs, enables your blood to pump with less effort, and tones your muscles—all of which can jump-start your metabolism. When you do jumping jacks, the exercise triggers your brain to release some feel-good chemicals into the bloodstream. If you get tired, try doing sets of five or ten, and then rest. Or better yet, add lunges or squats to vary the routine and keep those metabolic fires burning.

208. Get a Trampoline

Bouncing on a trampoline strengthens your legs, increasing their ability to serve as an auxiliary pump for your cardiovascular system, while increasing your pulse for a cardio workout. It also strengthens your voluntary and involuntary muscular system, which helps the entire system work more efficiently and burn more calories. It's also low-impact and spares wear and tear on your joints, feet, knees, and hips. Buy a minitrampoline to use when you're watching TV.

CHAPTER 14
Boost Your Metabolism by . . .
ADDING STRENGTH TRAINING

209. Understand Why You Need to Up the Ante

You already know that exercise is one big key to boosting metabolism. But, the bad news is that just engaging in aerobic exercise isn't enough. This is because when you engage in aerobic exercise your body craves energy for fuel and sometimes this means dipping into muscle proteins to get it. The result is a loss in muscle mass. To prevent this from happening and to assure that you are losing fat not muscle, you need to strength-train—either against your own body weight or with weights—at least twice a week. This extra work will also help boost your metabolism because every extra pound of muscle you put on burns 35 calories each day; each pound of fat only burns 2 calories. As we continue in this chapter, you'll learn about some great strength-training exercises that will boost your metabolism and give you that toned body you're looking for.

210. Strength-Train to Keep Those Metabolic Fires Burning

Eventually (if it hasn't happened already) your metabolism will slow down and eating pints of ice cream will have an effect on your waistline. As you grow older, you start to lose muscle mass, which leads to a larger body fat percentage. To bring this down, you'll need to incorporate strength training two to three times a week into your schedule to maintain your muscle mass and counteract the effects of aging so that you can keep your metabolism burning at an ideal rate.

Muscles require more energy (and also burn more calories) than fat cells.

211. Strength-Train for Overall Fitness

Aerobic activity is good, but to achieve total body fitness it's important to develop your body in different areas. These include:

- Muscular fitness, strength, and endurance
- Flexibility
- Cardiovascular endurance
- Body composition

Body composition describes the percentages of fat, bone, and muscle within your body; acceptable levels of body fat differ between the genders. For instance, an acceptable body fat percentage for a female who is not a professional athlete is 21–24 percent while for men the range is 14–17 percent. To make sure that you are achieving total body fitness, and also helping prevent heart disease and adult-onset diabetes, it is important to add strength training to your workout schedule.

212. Know Your Health Risks Before Beginning

Before you begin a strength-training program, it's important to see your doctor if you have a history of heart disease, diabetes, carpal tunnel syndrome, or high blood pressure, or you are over forty. Your doctor will recommend what level of activity is best for you so you can work out efficiently without putting your body in danger.

213. Slow Your Workout

When you work with weights, don't rush the process. In fact, with every rep, count to three as you lower the weight back to the start position. Slowing things down increases the breakdown of muscle tissue, which may sound counterproductive, but it's not. The muscle repair process that takes place following your workouts is what pumps up your metabolism for as long as 72 hours after your session. Don't go too easy on yourself though! Make sure you use weights that are heavy enough to make those final few reps a real struggle.

214. Focus on Your Core Muscles

Your core muscles are the abdominal muscles that do the heavy lifting in your life. Strengthening your core muscles is essential to building a strong muscular system, which also improves your ability to burn calories quicker and more efficiently. The abdominals are comprised of the rectus abdominus, the obliques, and the transverse abdominus. The rectus abdominus runs from your rib cage past your belly button, down into your pubic crest. This muscle can be contracted by bringing your hips closer to your rib cage, as you do in regular crunches. The external and internal obliques run in a more diagonal pattern and are located on each side of the rectus abdominus. The obliques are responsible for trunk rotation (twisting) and lateral bending. The transverse abdominus is the deepest abdominal muscle. It is commonly referred to as a stabilizing belt for your trunk and spine. This muscle is not responsible for movement, but it is a vital component to lower back health. These muscles combine with those of the lower back to form what is commonly referred to as the core.

215. Strengthen Your Core

Activities like martial arts, dancing, soccer, gymnastics, swimming, boxing, and basketball all require you to engage your core regularly. All of these options force you to twist and bend at the waist a lot, which is great work for your core muscles. The elliptical machine and the stationary bicycle do not do as much to strengthen your core. When you plan out your exercise regime, make sure you include abdominal strength-training exercises for 5 to 20 minutes every other day. Your mission is to choose a variety of exercises that work each core muscle in a challenging way. Start slowly and progress to extremely challenging exercises. How will you know if a certain exercise is extremely challenging? Give it a try and you'll find out. The exercises that you cannot already do will be the ones you should strive to accomplish.

216. Get Off on the Right Foot

When you begin strength training, or any other excise, take some commonsense precautions to protect your health and maximize the benefits:

- Start slowly and work your way up. It's natural to want to reach your maximum capacity as quickly as possible, but you have to be realistic; a gradual increase in weight or repetitions is the safest way to go. This is particularly true if you live a relatively sedentary lifestyle and are just beginning a serious exercise regimen.
- Always warm up for 5 to 10 minutes before engaging in strenuous exercise, and always cool down afterward.

128

- Drink plenty of fluids before, during, and after you exercise. This keeps your body functioning at full capacity and prevents dehydration.
- Maintain a safe pace. Here's a good rule of thumb: If you can't speak while exercising, you need to slow down.

217. Start with Dumbbells

If you're starting as a complete beginner, the best weights to use are dumbbells, which you can buy at a sporting goods store. Dumbbells are convenient, portable, and not overwhelming. You can use them while watching television or talking on the phone. They come in various weights, and you'll need a few so you can use different ones to work different muscles. If the only upper-body work you've done is lifting utensils to eat and drink, you probably want to start out with 3-pound weights. You'll graduate to 5 pounds in a few weeks and may be ready to work with 10-pound weights in a few months.

You may also want to purchase weights for lower-body work. A handy type of weight to use for leg strengthening is the kind that goes around your ankle and is adjusted with a Velcro strap.

218. Learn Strength-Training Basics

There are two ways to hold your dumbbells: overhand and underhand. For the overhand grip, grab the dumbbell with your palm facing down and knuckles facing up. For the underhand grip, your palm should be facing up and your knuckles down.

There are two ways to stand as well. One is with your feet shoulder-width apart, head and shoulders level, back erect, and knees slightly bent. This is the standard position. The other stance is bent over, feet shoulder-width apart, with one leg slightly extended. The idea is to work with a flat back and with your nonworking arm resting on the same-side thigh.

219. Ease into Strength Training

When first beginning a strength-training program, you should only perform one set of each exercise for the first couple of weeks, doing 12 to 15 repetitions (reps) per exercise. After this, you may increase to two or three sets after one warm-up set. If you could go well beyond 15–20 reps, increase the weight on your next set or at your next session; don't feel overwhelmed and think you must increase the number of sets to reap strength-training benefits.

220. Do Lunges

Stand with your feet shoulder-width apart, a dumbbell in each hand in the overhand grip. Step out with your right leg about one stride, landing on your heel and rolling your foot down flat against the floor. Bend both knees so that your right thigh is parallel to the floor (do not let your right knee go beyond your right foot). Your left thigh will be perpendicular to it, and your left heel will lift off the floor. Your arms remain by your sides during the exercise. Return to the starting position by rolling off the ball of your right foot. Alternate legs as you do your reps.

221. Do Leg Extensions

Choose a chair with firm back support and in which, when you're sitting, your feet rest flat on the floor. Sitting in the chair, put the ankle weights on both ankles. One leg at a time, squeezing with your thigh, lift your leg until your knee is straight. Control the descent. This is one rep.

222. Do Leg Curls

Lie on the floor on your stomach, with your arms at your side and the weights around your ankles. Turn your head to one side and lift both feet toward your buttocks, bringing your heels as close to your buttocks as you can. Use your abs to keep your hips pressing into the floor and lower your legs to the starting position for one rep.

223. Do Biceps Curls and Triceps Kickbacks

From the standing position with your arms at your sides, hold the dumbbell with an underhand grip. With your elbow securely against your side, raise (curl) the dumbbell up and toward your chest as far as it will go, and then control the weight as you bring your hand back down. This is one repetition. Alternate arms after each set.

For the triceps kickback, use an overhand grip; in the bent-over position, extend the working arm straight behind you (kick it back) without hyperextending your arm. Control the weight as you bend your arm back toward your chest. This is one repetition.

224. Do Front Raises and Shoulder Presses

The front raise works your deltoids. In the standing position with the dumbbell in an overhand grip, let both arms rest in front of your body so that your palms are resting on your thighs. Then lift one arm straight up to shoulder height so that it's parallel to the floor. Control the weight on the way back to the starting position for one repetition.

For the shoulder press, stand with the dumbbells in an overhand grip and bend your arms so that the dumbbells are by your ears, palms facing away from your body. Extend your arm up and slightly in front of your head; then lower to the starting position for one rep.

225. Do Bent-Over Rows

From the bent-over position, hold the dumbbell in an overhand grip and extend your arm toward the floor in a diagonal line from your shoulder. As if you are rowing a boat, bend your elbow and lift the dumbbell so that you use your back muscles as well as your arm muscles. Pretend you're starting a lawnmower but with a smoother action. Return to the starting position for one rep.

226. Do Pelvic Tilts

Lying on your back on the floor, preferably on a mat or folded towel for some cushion, bend your knees, rest your heels on the floor, and let your toes point up. Keep your arms at your side. Imagine gravity pulling your bellybutton onto the floor so that your lower back is flattened against the floor. This will cause your pelvis to rise slightly, and you should feel your abs tighten. Hold this position for several seconds, then relax and repeat. Do three sets of 10 reps.

227. Do Abdominal Crunches

Lie on your back with your knees bent and feet flat on the floor, about shoulder-width apart. Bring your arms up and put your hands under your head, thumbs pointing toward your ears. Don't interlock your fingers, even if your fingers overlap. Keep your head extended from your body so that your chin isn't digging into your chest. Start raising your trunk, curling up from your spine. Use your abs—not your hands—to pull yourself up.

Keep your elbows to the side and raise yourself up only enough to lift your shoulder blades off the floor. Pause and then bring your trunk back into position slowly for one repetition. Start by doing three sets of 15 reps, adjusting according to whether it feels like too much or not enough.

To increase the intensity of your workout, try doing your reps with your legs off the floor, crossed at your ankles. Keep your knees bent and your butt on the floor.

228. Play Ball

Get yourself a fitness ball and get to work toning and strengthening. A typical fitness ball is made of elastic rubber and comes in different sizes, from 14 inches to 34 inches in diameter when fully inflated. Unless you are very large or very small, you should probably choose a ball that is 26 inches in diameter. Fitness balls should not be confused with medicine balls, which are smaller but considerably heavier (up to 25 pounds).

229. Use a Ball to Do Pushups

Fitness ball pushups are among the best exercises you can do for your strength training. Begin by putting your ball in the middle of the floor and assuming the pushup position with your legs atop the ball. Pushups are much more difficult in this position, so don't plan on doing your usual number the first time you try this. With your legs up on the ball, you are working your abdominal muscles a lot more than with standard pushups, and you are also working the lower half of your body as you fight to maintain balance in that position.

230. Try a Modified Pushup

Here's another fitness-ball workout. Assume pushup position, with your feet up on the ball behind you. Instead of doing a pushup, however, elevate your buttocks to form an inverted or upside-down V with your body. Return to pushup position. Start slowly with this exercise and try to work up to being able to do three sets of 12 repetitions.

231. Try the Over and Back Routine

Another good workout with your fitness ball is to lie on your back on the floor, putting the ball between your feet. Raise the ball up to the point that you can take it with your hands. Take the ball from between your feet and lower it to the floor behind your head. Then take the ball and raise it up again and take hold of it with your feet, lowering it to the floor. Start slowly with this exercise, perhaps 4 repetitions initially. Strive to be able to complete three sets of 12 repetitions. This will strengthen your abs and your shoulders.

232. Hire a Personal Trainer

One of the best ways to really get into a program is to hire a personal trainer. These days, most gyms have trainers who are only too happy to help you create the exercise regimen that's best for you and to help you through it. This ensures that you are exercising correctly and at the proper pace. A trainer will also be able to give you ideas for boosting your metabolism or dealing with trouble spots, weaknesses, or challenges. If you have a problem staying motivated, a personal trainer can be just the cheerleader—or taskmaster—you need to get all fired up about exercising.

CHAPTER 15
Boost your metabolism by . . .
PRACTICING INTERVAL TRAINING

233. Add Interval Training

Interval training, otherwise known as speed play, has been shown to be one of the most effective methods to rev up your metabolism and burn fat, especially around the abdomen. During this time of training, you alternate between intense and moderate exercises to engage the aerobic and anaerobic systems. When you're working out at close to your maximum potential, lactic acid builds up as your body depletes its available oxygen. Then, when you slow down, oxygen floods into your system, breaking down the lactic acid and turning carbohydrates into energy. As you add more interval-training to your routine, your body will become more efficient at bringing oxygen to your muscles and burning fat. One way to incorporate this type of working out into your routine is by walking for 2 minutes and then running for 2 minutes and then walking again for 2 minutes, and so on. In this chapter, we'll provide a variety of exercises that are great for improving heart health and boosting metabolism. You can use all of them to develop a fun interval-training routine.

234. Stick with One Sport and Ramp Up the Intensity

In an Australian study, female volunteers either rode a stationary bike for 40 minutes at a steady pace or for 20-minute intervals, alternating 8 seconds of sprints and 12 seconds of easy pedaling. After 15 weeks, those who incorporated the sprints into their cardio workouts had lost three times as much body fat, including thigh and core flab, compared with those who exercised at a steady pace. Bursts of speed may stimulate a fat-burning response within the muscles, says lead researcher Ethlyn Gail Trapp, PhD.

Whether you ride, run, or row, try ramping things up to rev your burn: Start by doing three 8-seconds all-out, can't-talk sprints with 12 seconds at an easy pace between each effort. Work your way up until you can do 10 sprints over 20 minutes.

235. Choose Another Sport and Cross-Train

Cross-training is when you do more than one sport during your workouts. It adds variety to your workouts and decreases the chance of burnout. Cross-training also offers opportunities to exercise muscles not being utilized in your primary exercise, and allows muscles used more frequently an opportunity to rest and rejuvenate. Cross-training, of course, helps you keep active every day and provides an extra way to burn fat and boost your metabolism. There are many varieties of exercise available, some of which we'll discuss next.

236. Take a Kickboxing Class

Release some of that aggression in a kickboxing class where you'll learn to combine martial arts kicks with boxing punches for a great workout. There are many different styles of kickboxing and variants to choose from, including Brazilian jiujitsu, Muai Thai, Burmese kickboxing, American kickboxing, Indian adithada, and French savate, to name a few. Many of the kickboxing forms and styles have evolved into national and international competitions. As a kickboxer, you typically "fight" in rounds of varying duration (these are usually agreed upon prior to the fight). You get a great cardio workout regardless of the form of kickboxing you choose, and when you study it with a spouse or a friend you can practice (and get in shape) together.

237. Go Swimming

Oh, go jump in a lake. No, really. Swimming is one of the best exercises you can do. It provides a total-body workout but is also low-impact so it won't hurt your joints as it improves stamina and flexibility. Although your maximum heart rate may be up to 30 beats lower when you're working out in the water, you're still burning a significant amount of calories and your lungs are taking in more oxygen than if you were resting and that helps burn fat.

238. Try an Egrometer Workout

One popular cross-training machine is the egrometer, or rowing machine. As scullers have known for centuries, rowing is a terrific all-body exercise, strengthening your back, buttocks, and legs and developing your shoulders and arms. Rowing involves a two-stroke movement referred to as the drive and the recovery, which together produce a smooth and continuous action. It's important to follow good form on a rowing machine, so make sure you ask your health club to show you how to use it properly. This is another highly beneficial activity to do on a rest day. It strengthens the hips, buttocks, and upper body while sparing your legs.

239. Get on the NordicTrack

Another machine that provides a great upper- and lower-body workout is the NordicTrack. The NordicTrack and other machines that simulate cross-country skiing can be very effective in improving your coordination and balance while they work to increase your stamina, build muscles, and improve your overall aerobic fitness.

240. Use the Elliptical Trainer

For those of you who hate the treadmill, but want a full-body workout on an aerobic machine, check out the elliptical trainer. By combining cross-country skiing with climbing stairs and walking, the machine is able to provide an excellent cardiovascular workout without hurting your joints. The motion works all of the major muscle groups in your legs and offers the option to move backward and really focus on those glutes. Another great benefit of the machine is that you can adjust the program to your strength level, which allows both beginners and more advanced athletes to get a solid workout as they increase the resistance.

CHAPTER 16

Boost Your Metabolism by . . .

GOING FOR A RUN

241. Ease into a Running Program

You're ready to burn significant calories. You've been walking for weeks and you think you're ready to start running. Great!

We commend your efforts to boost your metabolism. But don't open the door and take a 5-mile jog or run around your neighborhood. Trust us, you'll be sore for days and you may even injure yourself. Running, unlike walking or some other aerobic activities, is a high-impact sport. It forces you to work harder than you're used to, which boosts your metabolism. If you haven't been active in some time, you may want to consider getting your doctor's approval before beginning. If that isn't a concern, we still recommend you start slowly, by integrating runs into your walks or by running very short distances—like a quarter or half mile—at a time. Eventually, as you start to get stronger and gain endurance, you'll naturally start running longer distances at a pace suitable for your body. In the chapter that follows, we'll help you set up a mileage base and work toward your goal.

242. Build Up a Mileage Base

Without question, safely building a mileage base, or the distance you run per week, is the most important area to focus on when beginning a running program. It's essential to begin running in small increments and build on these, no matter how silly or short your distance seems. Trying to take on too much too soon can greatly increase your chances of incurring an overuse injury and may ruin your appetite for running.

243. Follow the 10 Percent Rule

When you're ready to run for longer distances, increase your weekly mileage by 10 percent at a time. While it will take more time for you to reach your distance goal, you'll prevent an injury that could derail your progress.

244. Adhere to Running Principles

Don't push yourself to run fast right away. That is how many beginners burn out. Instead, concentrate on comfort and form. The way to approach running as a new way of life is to learn the right habits and then perfect them. After you've been running for a few months, it's a good idea to ask an experienced runner or (preferably) a coach to point out and correct your form flaws or deficiencies. This advice will improve your overall mechanics and running efficiency.

245. Stretch Your Muscles after You Run

A major misconception about running is that you must stretch beforehand. In fact, the opposite is the case: You should stretch after a workout. If you really feel you should stretch because you want to loosen up or warm up your muscles before the serious work, jog or walk for 5 to 10 minutes and then stretch. Start your run very slowly, and then ease into a training pace 5 to 10 minutes later. The idea is not to stretch a cold muscle. If you're planning a speed workout or race, jog for about a mile, stretch, and then do the speed workout or race. Don't stretch past the point of slight discomfort. If your muscles are still cold, don't try to stretch them like a rubber band, especially if you haven't run in a while. And don't bounce! Doing so can cause injuries.

246. Sign Up for a Race

If you're having trouble exercising as frequently as you should even after you've built up a substantial mileage base and are used to running regularly, sign up for a race! Choose a race that you're not presently prepared to participate in, but one that won't push you too far too fast, and then officially sign up. Once you've paid the fee, you'll be more likely to force yourself into training for it and reaching that finish line!

247. Don't Do the Marathons until You're Primed

You shouldn't even think of training for a marathon (26.2 miles) until you meet certain criteria. Specifically, you should have been running consistently four to five days per week, 25 miles per week, for at least a year (without any major injuries).

248. Run to Increase Endorphins

A well-known training effect is the production of endorphins. Endorphins are natural morphine-like hormones that produce a sense of well-being and reduce stress levels. They make you feel good and improve your mood. You may have heard of the "runner's high" associated with long-distance runners, but this group doesn't have exclusive rights to endorphin production. You, too, can produce your own endorphins through regular running exercise. The higher your level of endorphins, the less likely you are to use food for comfort. Also, the more endorphins you have in your system, the less stressed out you're likely to be, leading to a higher metabolism!

249. Alternate Running with Other Activities

Although running is excellent for building endurance, burning calories, and building strong bones and muscles, it is also hard on the joints. That's why it's important to alternate running with other aerobic activities so that you don't cause a musculoskeletal injury from overuse. Listen to your own body and its needs, but we recommend taking a few rest days to let yourself recover, especially if you're starting to run longer distances or if you're new to it altogether.

250. Try Jogging

Running is the act of moving quickly as you alternate feet. While it provides a great aerobic workout, it requires a lot of endurance. If you're not quite ready for that level of intensity, jogging is a slower version that provides the same benefits. If you can add five to six 30-second jogs to your walking routine, you'll find that you'll start to increase your overall endurance and burn more calories.

CHAPTER 17

Boost Your Metabolism by . . .

LEADING AN ACTIVE LIFESTYLE

Keep Moving to Help Expend Energy

Take the Stairs Whenever You Can

Park as Far Away as You Can

Run Errands on Your Lunch Break

Take a Stretch Break

Get Off Your Duff

Work Out While Watching TV

Buy Some Workout Duds

Ask a Friend to Join You in a Fitness Program

Take a Walk

Walk 10,000 Steps a Day

Walk to the Local Market

Dance the Night Away

Decide on a Dance

Go Horseback Riding

Join a Bowling League

Take Diving Lessons

Coach a Children's Sports Team

Choose an Active Vacation

Make Fitness Your Destination

Take an Adventure Vacation

Make Any Vacation an Active One

Build a House with Habitat for Humanity

Adopt and Regularly Walk a Rescued Dog

251. Keep Moving to Help Expend Energy

Remember: If you're not moving, your metabolism is not revving! Being sedentary can be the worst thing for your internal engine. By being active in small ways throughout your day, you're helping to keep your metabolism cranking. If you have a job that keeps you in your seat for hours during the day, be sure to get up and move around frequently. If you come home from the grocery store with several bags, try taking several trips from the car to your front door. You'll find that when you shun the "couch potato" mentality and make the effort to be a little more active, you're adopting a healthy habit that's hard to break!

252. Take the Stairs Whenever You Can

Climbing stairs quickly elevates your heart rate for a metabolic jolt that burns 8 calories per minute, approximately twice as much as you'll burn taking a brisk walk. If there are stairs where you work, take a few breaks throughout the day—5–10 minutes each—and climb as many stairs as you can. If your energy slumps after lunch, boost it—and your metabolism—by leaping up for a stair climb.

253. Park as Far Away as You Can

If your office is located in a good area for walking, take advantage of this natural way to slip in an extra 20 to 30 minutes of exercise a day. Park far away whenever you are shopping at a grocery store or a mall. In fact, while in the mall, take a few spins around at a brisk pace, and you'll rev up your heart and your metabolism.

254. Run Errands on Your Lunch Break

Lunchtime is the perfect time of day for a burst of energetic hustle. Plan your workday so you can take at least 30 minutes to run errands—and then literally run, or at least walk briskly. Every time you hustle, walk briskly, or run instead of walk, you not only burn more calories, but ensure that your metabolism stays cranked up for a longer time.

255. Take a Stretch Break

Stretching is an excellent way to reduce stress and give your metabolism a boost in the middle of a day when you can't get away and exercise. Take 5 or 10 minutes to do basic stretches for each of the large muscle groups and make sure to breathe deeply as you do—as you would in yoga—to provide your body with extra oxygen so it can burn more fat.

256. Get Off Your Duff

If you have a sedentary job, it's vitally important that you find ways to move your body at work. When someone in another department needs a file, jump up and dash over to deliver it. If you needed something duplicated, take it to the copier and then do a few deep-knee bends while you are waiting. The best way to combat a sedentary job and boost your metabolism is to find a multitude of ways to get off your duff and move your body. Walk briskly, toss in some toe-touches, work on some waist whittlers, or do whatever you can think of to move and stretch your muscles.

257. Work Out While Watching TV

Television time doesn't have to be a bad thing, as long as you're not sitting in front of the TV while you should be working out. Instead, do both! Fill a basket with weights, resistance bands, a yoga mat, and a jump rope and place it near your flat screen. Instead of sinking into your sofa and loafing while you watch your favorite show, use those opportunities to do mini-workouts.

258. Buy Some Workout Duds

A common thread amongst fitness success stories is that they all dress for fitness no matter what. Even after a hard day's work, these people put on their workout gear to help get them in the mood. Being motivated is an important factor in your journey to boost your metabolism. Buy yourself some snazzy workout clothes and see if you don't soon relish putting them on—and then do so often.

259. Ask a Friend to Join You in a Fitness Program

Once you have resolved to live a healthier lifestyle, invite a friend to be your exercise buddy. Walk during your lunch hour. Ride bikes or try in-line skating around a local park. Take a swim aerobics class. Do yoga together. The point is to make exercise a social event as much as a workout. When you are laughing and conversing, the time goes by much more quickly. Socializing stimulates the mind just as exercise increases blood flow. Both nourish you, help raise your metabolism, and should be part of a healthy lifestyle.

260. Take a Walk

One of the problems some of us have with physical activity is that it is too hard on our joints. One way to alleviate this problem is by using an elliptical trainer, but another is to engage in a low-impact sport such as walking or swimming. Although it may feel easy, walking is actually a great way to build muscular strength and endurance and improve your coordination. Long walks are best for getting the heart muscle working, but if they don't fit into your schedule, consider taking short walks—10 or 15 minutes at a time—throughout the day.

261. Walk 10,000 Steps a Day

Many people are now trying to ensure they take at least 10,000 steps per day, which has been shown to be a marker of good health. If you walk about 3.5 miles per hour, then you probably take somewhere between 5,000 and 7,000 steps in one hour, depending on your height (and, therefore, your stride length). You can walk that number of steps during a one-hour TV show just by marching in place. You'll burn about 150 to 250 calories during that hour. That may not sound like a lot, but if you're just watching TV without moving, you'll only burn about 40 to 60 calories, and not get any boost to your metabolism during that time. Do that for one hour a day for a year, and you'll burn off about 9 pounds!

262. Walk to the Local Market

If there's a grocery store or a weekend farmers' market in your neighborhood, gather together canvas or heavy-duty utility bags and head out for a brisk walk to do your grocery shopping. Since you'll be carrying the bags of groceries back home afterward, you'll want to be sure you can carry what you purchase, so buy only what will fit into a couple of bags. Walking while carrying groceries means you'll be burning a lot more calories than you would driving your car to the store. Plus, it's better for the environment. Now, that's something to feel good about.

263. Dance the Night Away

Even if you have two left feet, turn on your CD player or put your iPod in its docking station and start moving. Whether it's in your bedroom or your living room or a local club or studio, dancing is wonderful exercise. In fact, aerobics as a form of exercise began as an offshoot of jazz dance (sort of like New York City's Rockettes). Because you move quickly and use all of your limbs, you burn a ton of calories dancing. The funny thing about dancing, too, is that all you really need is a sense of rhythm and an enjoyment of music—you can be good at it no matter what your size or shape.

264. Decide on a Dance

Here's a list of different dance styles, their benefits, and their calorie-burning count for a moderate intensity for 30 minutes. Try these dances to work your body and boost your metabolism.

- **Ballroom dancing**: Burns 150 calories an hour. Strengthens leg, shoulder, ab, arm, back, and glute muscles; increases flexibility; improves concentration; only increases heart strength if you do fast steps, such as swing dancing

- **Ballet**: Burns 150 calories per hour. Strengthens leg, shoulder, ab, arm, back, and glute muscles; increases flexibility; does not increase cardio power (you need concentration and stamina)
- **Country line dancing**: Burns 125 calories an hour. Strengthens leg, shoulder, ab, arm, back, and glute muscles
- **Disco dancing**: Burns 175 calories an hour. Strengthens leg, shoulder, ab, arm, back, and glute muscles; strengthens the heart
- **Salsa dancing**: Burns 170 calories an hour. Strengthens leg, shoulder, ab, arm, back, and glute muscles; increases flexibility and strengthens the heart

265. Go Horseback Riding

Just imagine bundling up in a sweater and scarf on a chilly spring or fall morning and riding a horse along a beach past crashing waves or through a leafy forest glade, replete with dew-laden spiderwebs and small critters scurrying out of your path. The world looks and feels different from the back of a horse. Horseback riding seems to heighten the senses of sight, smell, and touch. Riding at full gallop requires the use of those thigh muscles and feet and hands to stay in the saddle. Mounting and dismounting also can provide a little workout. But the joy of sitting atop a horse and observing the world awakening is a bonus for doing horseback riding as an exercise.

266. Join a Bowling League

You might not know that the ancient Egyptians enjoyed a good game of bowling. Of course, their balls were stone and players at opposite ends of

BOOST YOUR METABOLISM BY . . . **LEADING AN ACTIVE LIFESTYLE**

the lane threw their balls (a big one and a smaller one) at the same time. Today many bowling leagues are looking for a few good participants. Of course, you can bowl alone if that makes you happy, but many people believe that bowling is a game best enjoyed in the company of family or friends. Getting out for a few hours of bowling is good for shifting the constant pressures of home and work and decreasing stress levels while strengthening your friendships by engaging in pleasurable activities with your bowling partners.

267. Take Diving Lessons

You've dreamed of seeing coral reefs, sunken treasure ships, and the beautiful world that lies beneath the surface of the ocean. What's keeping you from making your dream a reality? Dive shops often have dive instructors who will teach you the basics in a swimming pool. Then you'll take day trips to the ocean or a body of water where you can put what you've learned to work. Divers watch out for each other and the friendships can continue long after the dive is over. Find the time, money, and the courage to go after your dreams. On the other side of achieving them, you'll feel pleasure and gratification and have a few new friends. And you'll lose lots of weight!

268. Coach a Children's Sports Team

If you have children, you already know how much they love to run while playing games in the yard or at school. You can help them develop an appreciation for teamwork and good sportsmanship by coaching their team in T-ball, soccer, gymnastics, synchronized swimming, football, track and field, or other sports. Children are naturally happy and enthusiastic. Volunteer to serve as their coach and share in their joy when they play. You may discover that winning or losing really isn't as important as how they play the game.

269. Choose an Active Vacation

Take an active vacation, with no goal other than to enjoy yourself and have fun. There are spas with a fitness focus, resorts with activities (skiing, swimming, and skating), walking vacations, biking trips, hiking treks, and far more adventurous options, such as mountain climbing, backwoods cross-country snowshoeing, kayaking, trips during which you learn to sail, and other skill-focused adventures. Whatever your choice, be sure to bring the equipment requested and the right shoes so that you'll be comfortable and able to take part in all the activities.

270. Make Fitness Your Destination

When you plan your next vacation, consider centering it around physical activity. Build hiking or kayaking or even mountain climbing into your plans or look for an organized event you can participate in. Here are some planned events that offer the opportunity to visit new places, be active in the great outdoors, and meet new people while having fun.

- Bay to Breakers, San Francisco, California
- Bike Ride Around Lake Tahoe, Lake Tahoe, California

- Gasparilla Distance Classic, Tampa, Florida
- Peachtree Road Race, Atlanta, Georgia
- Run to the Far Side, San Francisco, California

271. Take an Adventure Vacation

For bold travelers, there's nothing more exciting than an adventure vacation. Not only do you get to experience a place you've never seen before, but you also get to challenge yourself physically and keep in shape. This type of vacation can go in many directions. Are you interested in biking? Perhaps you'd like to bike through France, stopping at hostels along the way. Do you like running in races? Why not follow a trail of 5K races all over New England in the spring? Here are some other ideas that might fulfill your adventurous whims.

- Walk the outback of Australia.
- Learn to surf in Hawaii.
- Learn to sail in the British Virgin Islands.
- Bicycle through Baja California.
- Hike to Machu Picchu.
- Helihike in British Columbia.

The important thing to remember about these trips is that they require training. Even if you're very active, you need to train specifically for the type of trip you're going to take. Ask the group you're going with to advise you on ways you can get in shape to get the most out of your trip.

272. Make Any Vacation an Active One

While adventurous vacations are lots of fun and give you great memories, they can take a lot of planning and money. If you don't have the means or the stamina for such a vacation, don't worry! You can turn almost any vacation into a fitness vacation with just a few easy additions. The following is a list of things you should consider taking with you on your trip, although, of course, the exact list will depend on your location and activity:

- Bathing suit, towel, bathing cap, goggles
- Exercise bands
- Exercise DVDs
- iPod with downloaded workout programs
- Sneakers
- Workout clothes, including bike shorts
- Yoga mat

Finally, if you want to consider luxury with fitness, consider fitness spas! Spas used to be associated with weight loss and deprivation, but now they have accepted and embraced the knowledge that fitness is an essential part of health, weight loss, and relaxation. Spas will encourage you to hike, swim, lift weights, and do Pilates and yoga, and you can do any of these things in Arizona, Tennessee, or Provence!

273. Build a House with Habitat for Humanity

Swing a hammer, carry some lumber, and help build a home for a poor family if this appeals to your social conscience. Habitat for Humanity (*www.habitat.org*) is a nonprofit organization that works in tandem with volunteers in communities worldwide to build houses for low-income people. Former president Jimmy Carter and his wife spend a week every year swinging hammers to help erect affordable shelter for the poor on behalf of Habitat for Humanity. If you believe that you could be doing more to help the less fortunate, then grab your hammer, get out there, and work up a sweat with—and for—people like yourself.

274. Adopt and Regularly Walk a Rescued Dog

Animal shelters all over America often have more animals than they can properly care for, meaning that some animals' lives will end there. You can make a difference by choosing to adopt a pet from a shelter. Regular exercise keeps your animal—and you!—trim, agile, limber, and mentally alert. Physical exercise improves his joint health as well. Take him to the dog park where he can play with other dogs, too, because dog experts say it is good for his socialization skills. If your dog belongs to one of the larger breeds such as a Labrador or German shepherd, leaving him in your backyard does not guarantee that he will exercise on his own. Take the time to exercise together as part of your daily routine. Whether you're walking, jogging, or swimming together, think of it as happy bonding.

CHAPTER 18
Boost Your Metabolism by . . .
CONTROLLING FAT INTAKE

275. Understand Fats

The food science that centers around fat is simple. Fats are simply chains of carbon molecules bonded with hydrogen molecules and attached to a glycerol molecule. There are three kinds of fat: saturated, monounsaturated, and polyunsaturated. These terms define the type of bonds that the carbon molecules form with one another and with the hydrogen molecules.

Carbon molecules can bond with four other molecules in various formations. In saturated fats, all the carbon molecules are singly bonded to each other and with two hydrogen molecules. In monounsaturated fats, one of the carbon-to-carbon bonds is a double bond without two hydrogen molecules. In polyunsaturated fats, there are two or more double-bonded carbon molecules.

When hydrogen is introduced into a polyunsaturated fat, the hydrogen molecules begin to bond with the double-bonded carbon molecules. If they line up on the same side of the chain, the configuration is called *cis*. If the hydrogen molecules line up on opposite sides of the chain, the configuration is called trans. Heat and pressure force the hydrogen molecules to line up in the trans configuration.

In the cis configuration, which is the natural form of mono- and polyunsaturated fats, the positioning of the hydrogen molecules makes a kink in the chain. As a result, they cannot pack closely together, so the fat will remain liquid at room temperature. In the trans configuration, the hydrogen molecules pair up on opposite sides of the carbon molecules. This positioning straightens out the chain, so the molecules pack closely together, making a fat that is solid or semisolid at room temperature.

Unlike fiber-filled foods that move quickly through your system, 95 percent of consumed fat is absorbed into your body. This high absorption rate means that almost every bit of fat that you eat stays with you, causing weight gain and a slow metabolism if you eat more than your body can handle. In this chapter, you'll learn about the various types of fat commonly found in the foods you eat and how to avoid the fat trap—keeping your metabolism high and your body healthy!

276. Learn How to Read Fat Content Labeling

Food labeling will definitely help you identify fat content, but you need to understand the rules of labeling to really know if what you are reading is an accurate reflection of the item's fat content. According to U.S. government regulations, foods containing less than 0.5 gram of fat per serving are called fat-free, which sounds great. If, however, you eat three or four servings, trace fat content adds up. Also, the more generic labels give 3 grams of fat or less per serving the title *low-fat*. Products containing at least 25 percent less fat than the original version earn the title *reduced fat*.

277. Beware of Hidden Trans Fat

Just because something is listed as having 0 percent trans fat, doesn't necessarily mean that it is completely trans-fat free. In terms of labeling, it's important to note that trans fat may not be listed. If the words *partially hydrogenated*, *margarine*, or *shortening* appear in the ingredients list, the product contains some artificial trans fat. Ingredients are listed in decreasing amounts, so if the hydrogenated fat or shortening appears toward the beginning of the list, each serving probably has close to 0.5 gram of trans fat. If it appears toward the end of the list, there are probably close to 0 or 0.1 gram of trans fat per serving. If you purchase and eat processed foods, look for the phrase *no trans fat*. In this labeling, *zero* doesn't mean zero, but *no* means what it says.

Labels sometimes use the terms *partially hydrogenated* and *hydrogenated* interchangeably, so avoid products that use either phrase. The words *esterification* or *esterified* are also red flags indicating fats that have been manipulated with chemicals.

278. Don't Abandon All Fats

Even though you hear a lot of bad things about fat, it is a necessary nutrient when consumed in the right amounts. Fat helps supply energy for aerobic exercise in the form of fatty acids and may help you lose weight. Fat also protects your organs by insulating them against the cold, helps to make cell walls permeable so that necessary nutrients can flow between the cells and the blood, and serves as a building block for hormones. It is important to keep fats in your diet but to eat the right types in limited quantities.

279. Choose Good Fats

Medium-chain saturated fats, like those found in coconut oil, need very little processing by the body to be absorbed and used. They are quickly metabolized in the liver and aren't stored in the body. These fats are a good source of quick energy and do not contribute to heart disease; in fact, they may protect against inflammation in the body. Medium-chain saturated fats also have antimicrobial properties.

Rice bran oil, avocado oil, flaxseed oil, nut oils, grapeseed oil, and extra-virgin olive oil are all good choices. Browse through a natural-foods store or food co-op and really look at the oils lining their shelves. Read labels and browse the Internet for information about these fats and oils.

280. Understand Unsaturated Fats

Unsaturated fats—when consumed in moderation—can be good for you as well. In fact, some, like the omega-3 fatty acids found in fish can help the heart and even lead to an increase in weight loss. Unsaturated fats come in four varieties: monounsaturated, polyunsaturated, omega-3 fatty acids, and trans fats. Trans fats should be avoided, but the other three types help by lowering LDL cholesterol levels and decreasing the risk of heart attacks. Monounsaturated fat is found in olive and canola oil, nuts, and avocados; polyunsaturated fats are found in fish, peanut butter, and some seeds.

281. Understand Saturated Fats

Saturated fats—or "bad fats"—are the major dietary cause of high cholesterol. They are found in animal foods and products (like beef, pork, ham, and sausage); dairy products, especially whole dairy products (like whole milk, cheese, cream, and ice cream); and oils (like cottonseed oil and palm kernel oils). These fats are typically solid at room temperature.

282. Understand Natural Trans Fat

Naturally occurring trans fat is made when bacteria in the stomach of ruminant animals (cows and sheep) transform some of the fats found in plant material into the trans configuration. This means that products like milk, cheese, cream, beef, and lamb have small amounts of naturally occurring trans fat. Unlike artificial trans fat, these natural fats are actually good for you. In your body, they are transformed into CLA, or conjugated linoleic acid, which has a positive effect on heart function. CLAs also help protect against free-radical damage to cells, which helps boost your metabolism and protect you from developing cancer (especially of the breast and colon).

283. Understand Artificial Trans Fat

Trans fat is an artificial fat produced when liquid vegetable oil is treated with heat, chemicals, and hydrogen to transform it into a product that is semisolid at room temperature. The artificial trans fat that is causing all the uproar is made from partially hydrogenated polyunsaturated oil, usually soybean or cottonseed oil. To partially hydrogenate oil, the liquid oil is combined with a metal catalyst to speed up the chemical reaction. Hydrogen gas is bubbled through the mixture under high temperature and pressure, and the fat is then steam-cleaned and deodorized. All of these steps result in a highly processed, artificial food that is treated as a natural fat source by the body.

The fat is inexpensive, performs beautifully in both baked and deep-fried applications, keeps food fresher longer, and provides a nice "mouthfeel" to many products. Trans fat was a godsend to the food industry. It was used instead of animal fats like butter or lard because those fats are notoriously volatile. They become rancid quickly, are difficult to store, and can be very expensive. Hydrogenated fat is easier to work with, doesn't become rancid, and can be used over and over again without breaking down or burning.

But, as always with something that seems too good to be true, there was a catch. Trans fat is one of the few food ingredients that is truly bad for you. Fortunately, many popular baking products, like Crisco, that once relied on trans fat are changing their recipes to ensure the health of their customers. These changes are good for your health and good for your metabolism!

284. Understand How Artificial Trans Fat Affects Your Body

Artificial trans fat isn't recognized by your body as an artificial substance, so it is not discarded in the digestion process. Instead, it is used in chemical reactions as though it was a normal fatty acid. In your cell membranes, in the lining of arteries and veins, and in your liver, brain, and kidneys, trans fat is fully incorporated, changing the functions and properties of your cells and of the enzymes that fuel your body. Sometimes knowing how something affects your body inspires you to eat healthier. Trans fat has been proven to affect our bodies negatively in the following ways:

- Changes hormone levels
- Increases LDL cholesterol levels
- Decreases HDL cholesterol levels

BOOST YOUR METABOLISM BY . . . **CONTROLLING FAT INTAKE**

- Damages cell membranes, decreasing nutrient absorption
- Reduces flexibility of capillaries and arteries
- Increases the level of insulin in the bloodstream
- Contributes to weight gain, especially around the midsection
- Causes inflammation in cell walls and artery walls
- Increases the risk of cancer through free radicals

285. Stay on the Low End of Fat Quotas

Every day, an average healthy person should consume approximately 2,000 calories. Of that amount, 45 to 65 should be from carbohydrates, 10 to 35 percent from protein, and 20 to 35 percent from fat. That means that 900 to 1300 calories should come from carbs, 200 to 700 calories from protein, and 400 to 700 calories from fat.

Try to keep trans fat consumption to less than 1 percent of your daily calories; that is about 2.0 grams. Saturated fat consumption should be no more than 20 to 30 grams per day. The total amount of cholesterol you should consume is around 200 to 300 milligrams.

286. Know Your Trans Fat Oils

The chart on the following page provides vital information about the amount of trans fat in common oils. Keep this in mind when you head to the grocery store and make the metabolism-boosting decision to avoid these fatty foods.

ARTIFICIAL TRANS FAT IN FATS AND OILS

Type of Fat	Amount of Artificial Trans Fat*	Serving Size
Corn oil	0.04 grams	1 tablespoon
Canola oil	0.11 grams	1 tablespoon
Soybean oil	0.09 grams	1 tablespoon
Solid shortening	4.28 grams	1 tablespoon
Stick margarine	2.70 grams	1 tablespoon
Nonfat tub margarine	0.03 grams	1 tablespoon
80% fat tub margarine	1.10 grams	1 tablespoon

*Amounts were calculated using NutriBase Clinical version 7.0. When amounts were not available, all of the monounsaturated, polyunsaturated, and saturated fat numbers were added, and then subtracted from the total number of fat grams. The remainder is a good approximation of the trans fat in each product.

287. Cook at Home

One of the best things you can do to reduce your exposure to trans fat and limit excess fat in other food products is to cook more at home. Having control over the foods you put in your body is an important first step toward reclaiming your health—and boosting your metabolism. Using natural fats like butter, cold-pressed olive oil, and coconut oil will ensure that even your baked and fried foods will have little or no artificial trans fat.

You can substitute trans fat–free margarines specifically made for baking for the butter and use egg substitutes as well. Be sure to follow the directions for converting recipes on these products' packages.

288. Choose the Right Frying Oil

When you choose to fry or make a food that is higher in fat, use natural fats like butter or lard. Cold-pressed peanut oil and canola oil are also good choices for deep-frying.

289. Eat Brightly Colored Food

Base your diet on the color wheel. Food that is brightly colored automatically has less fat and will help boost your metabolic rate. Try eating brightly colored foods, like red bell peppers, strawberries, melons, tomatoes, blueberries, grapes, carrots, nuts, seeds, and legumes.

290. Choose Whole Foods over Processed Foods

Whole foods—meats and dairy products, whole grains, legumes, vegetables, and fruits—should form the bulk of your diet. However, keep in mind that totally banning any food group is going to eliminate some essential nutrients. The only really "bad" food is trans fat! In fact, nutritionists know that whole foods contain many vital micronutrients that haven't even been discovered. Eating processed foods and junk food and using a multivitamin to compensate isn't a viable option.

CHAPTER 19

Boost Your Metabolism by . . .

MANAGING YOUR MINERALS

291. Understand the Importance of Minerals

It's a little strange to think, isn't it, that the same minerals we see in rocks and in tall buildings are the keys to our body functioning like a well-oiled machine? Well, minerals are necessary to keep our bodies working at full capacity and if that doesn't happen, our metabolism takes a beating. While some minerals provide structure to our bones, others ensure that our muscles, heart, and nerves are working properly and are major factors in the metabolic process. There are fourteen essential minerals that are required for the body to work properly, and they must be consumed in our diet because we are unable to make them within our bodies. Unlike vitamins, which we will cover in Chapter 20, minerals do not contain carbon so they are known as inorganic compounds. In this chapter we'll cover all the essential minerals that do a body good.

292. Understand How Minerals Work

For minerals to work and help with the body's functions, they must be absorbed through the intestinal walls and then transported and stored in different types of cells. Some, like calcium, attach to proteins and build structure, while others, like potassium, are used in cells to regulate the balance of fluids. Since we only need trace amounts of most minerals, it is important to consult with your doctor before choosing to supplement your diet; large amounts of minerals may be toxic.

293. Know Why Potassium Is So Important

Potassium, an essential mineral and electrolyte, regulates the balance of fluids and minerals in cells and also works to maintain heart and kidney function and a healthy blood pressure. This mineral is also key to boosting your metabolism because it is required to make your muscles contract and because it helps convert blood sugar into glycogen. Glycogen is stored in your muscles and liver and later burned for energy. Though a potassium deficiency is uncommon, it can be caused by kidney disease, chronic diarrhea, vomiting, or the overuse of laxatives and diuretics. Good sources for the mineral include bananas, beans, spinach, sweet potatoes, papaya, and Swiss chard.

294. Choose Foods Rich in Potassium

A diet low in fat and cholesterol and rich in foods containing potassium, magnesium, and calcium—such as fruits, vegetables, legumes, and dairy foods—has shown evidence of reducing blood pressure. Potassium-rich foods include fresh meat, poultry, fish, figs, prunes, lentils, kidney beans, black beans, baked potatoes (with skin), avocados, orange juice, cantaloupes, bananas, and cooked spinach.

295. Eat Healthy Sources of Chloride

The mineral chloride is responsible for regulating the diffusion of body fluids through cell walls and functions as an electrolyte when it transmits electrical impulses through the water in the body. It aids in the metabolic process by combining with hydrogen in the stomach to produce hydrochloric acid, one of the most powerful digestive enzymes that breaks down the food we eat, and by helping to balance pH levels and the amount of carbon dioxide being expelled from the body. Chloride is in salt, but for a healthier option, choose kelp, olives, tomatoes, lettuce, and rye.

296. Reduce Your Sodium

Salt can make some foods taste better, but in the United States, we consume too much and we need to put down the salt shaker. Overconsumption can lead to osteoporosis, hypertension, edema, and even death. So for heart health and a faster metabolism, reduce your intake to no more than a teaspoon (2,300 milligrams) of salt a day. However, according to the 2005 Daily Guidelines published by the Department of Health and Human Services (HHS) and the Department of Agriculture (USDA), "Individuals with hypertension, blacks, and middle-aged and older adults should aim to consume no more than 1,500 mg of sodium per day."

297. Know Why Magnesium Is So Important

Even before reading this book, you probably knew it was important to get enough calcium, but did you know that getting enough magnesium is equally important? In fact, this macromineral is used to activate more than 300 enzymes as well as create the lattice-like structure within our bones. Magnesium plays a role in energy metabolism, helps metabolize fats, carbohydrates, and proteins and store fuel inside our muscles that can later be used for energy. Other benefits magnesium provides include preventing the onset of Alzheimer's disease, boosting the effectiveness of some antioxidants, and making sure that your neurons are firing properly. Aim for 350 milligrams a day.

298. Choose Foods Rich in Magnesium

Magnesium can be found in a wide variety of foods. The best sources include legumes, almonds, avocados, toasted wheat germ, wheat bran, fish, seafood, fruit, fruit juice, pumpkin seeds, and whole grains. Green vegetables, especially cooked spinach, can be good sources, too.

299. Don't Deplete Your Phosphorus

If your stress levels have caused you to stock up on antacids, you may want to consider supplementing your diet with phosphorus. This chemical element helps build strong bones and teeth, repair tissue, and build cell membranes (in the form of phospholipids), but it is also the primary regulator that transforms carbohydrates, proteins, and fats in the food you eat into energy and activates the B vitamins.

300. Protect Your Cells with Selenium, But Don't Go Overboard

This very powerful antioxidant benefits the body by preventing oxidation of fat. Why is this important? By inhibiting oxidation, selenium slows age-related brain deterioration and preserves cognitive function. Selenium also benefits the immune system, and some studies suggest that it improves circulation. Because selenium levels tend to decline with age, older people should take selenium supplements and add selenium-rich foods to their diets.

Selenium also works with glutathione peroxidase to keep dangerous free radicals under control. In Japan, where people traditionally consume about 500 micrograms of selenium a day, the cancer rate is nearly five times lower than in countries where daily selenium intake is less. There is no established RDA for selenium, although men and women can safely consume between 50 and 200 micrograms daily, not exceeding 400 micrograms per day for adults over eighteen.

Natural sources of selenium include broccoli, cabbage, celery, cucumbers, garlic, onions, kidneys, liver, chicken, whole-grain foods, seafood, and milk.

WARNING: Selenium can become toxic if more than 400 micrograms are consumed on a daily basis.

301. Get Plenty of Zinc

When your body is running low on zinc, your metabolism may slow down. That's because this mineral is one of the main regulators of blood sugar and carbohydrate levels, and without it, insulin levels can spike. Zinc also transports unnecessary carbon dioxide from tissues to the lungs, protects your sense of taste and smell, and assists with the products of RNA and DNA. If you prefer not to take a zinc supplement (which if you do, should not exceed 40 milligrams), you can dine on red meat, seeds, nuts, and wheat products. Women who are pregnant or breastfeeding may require more.

302. Increase Your Chromium Intake

Chromium helps the body metabolize fat, convert blood sugar into energy, and make insulin work more efficiently. Several recent studies have also shown that chromium protects the heart by lowering serum cholesterol levels and triglycerides. Sources rich in chromium include whole-grain foods, egg yolks, broccoli, orange juice, grape juice, seafood, dairy products, and many different types of meat. Individuals with Type 2 diabetes or who are pregnant have increased urinary excretion of chromium and may benefit from supplementation. Trivalent chromium, the form in most chromium supplements, is also extremely safe.

303. Indulge in Tryptophan (5-HTP)

Why is it that on Thanksgiving there aren't usually any squabbles after the standard turkey dinner? That's because everyone has just ingested the amino acid tryptophan, a neurotransmitter (a chemical that carries messages from the brain to the body) that is transformed into serotonin, which improves both mood and the ability to sleep.

Tryptophan also assists with metabolism, not just by improving stress levels but also by contributing to the production of niacin, which lowers "bad" cholesterol levels in the blood. Great sources of tryptophan include egg whites, cod, Parmesan cheese, chicken breast, fish, beef tenderloin, and of course, turkey.

304. Eat Copper-Rich Foods

Copper is found in all the tissues in the body, but it is concentrated in the brain, heart, kidney, and liver. It helps the body make hemoglobin (needed to carry oxygen to red blood cells) and red blood cells by aiding in the absorption of iron. Copper is part of many enzymes in the body and helps produce energy in cells, helping boost your metabolism. In addition, copper helps make hormones that regulate a variety of body functions, including heartbeat, blood pressure, and wound healing. Copper is found mostly in organ meats, especially liver, and in seafood, nuts, and seeds. It can also be found in poultry, legumes, and dark green leafy vegetables.

305. Eat Foods Rich in Iron

Iron is crucial to metabolism. It brings oxygen to the cells, strengthens the immune system, and is one of the building blocks of carnitine and other enzymes required for digestion. Though iron toxicity can be very dangerous, iron deficiency will cause your body to become fatigued because your cells won't be receiving the oxygen they need. Women need extra iron when they're menstruating because of the loss of blood, but because of the dangers of toxicity, we recommend eating foods rich in iron—such as soybeans, beans, tofu, beef, and spinach—over taking an iron supplement.

306. Take SAMe

SAMe (pronounced "Sammy") is a form of the amino acid methionine that occurs naturally in the body and is used for many essential functions, including stabilizing moods by increasing the levels of certain neurotransmitters; as a result, it may affect moods and emotions. In nine studies, SAMe compared favorably with antidepressant drugs, including imipramine, amitryptaline, and clomipramine. Some researchers have found that SAMe supplementation has improved mood disorders, without the side effects of other antidepressants (such as weight gain, headaches, sleep disturbances, and sexual dysfunction). And, SAMe works faster than some prescription antidepressants, often in four to ten days compared with two to six weeks for drugs. Also, it's much easier to exercise and make healthy food choices that boost our metabolism when we are feeling healthy and happy!

Note: SAMe is not recommended for pregnant women during their first trimester or for women who are breastfeeding.

CHAPTER 20
Boost Your Metabolism by . . .
TAKING YOUR VITAMINS

307. Understand Why You Need Vitamins

Vitamins are produced by living material such as plants and animals and are natural substances that are necessary for almost every process in the body. While vitamins do not provide calories or directly supply energy, they do help carbohydrates, proteins, and fats produce energy.

The micronutrients found in vitamins can help trigger thousands of chemical reactions that are essential to maintaining good health. Most of these reactions are linked because one reaction will trigger another. A missing vitamin or a deficiency of a certain vitamin anywhere in the linked chain can cause a collapse, leading to a slower metabolism. Remember, your body needs to be healthy and active to function properly; if it's not getting the vitamins it needs, your metabolism is guaranteed to slow down.

Most vitamins are not made by the body in sufficient amounts to maintain health and must instead be obtained through food. Vitamins are found in a wide variety of foods, and some foods are better sources than others. For this reason, eating a wide variety of foods ensures a better intake of vitamins. However, sometimes people don't get the vitamins they need through diet, which is why some supplementation is both safe and desirable.

308. Evaluate Your Need for Supplements

Before you head to the drugstore and drop every nutritional supplement you see into your cart, check to see if you're already doing enough on your own in the multivitamin department.

- Do you eat 6 to 11 servings of grains (bread, cereal, rice, pasta, and other grain foods)?
- Do you eat at least 3 servings of vegetables?
- Do you eat at least 2 servings of fruit?
- Do you eat 2 or more servings of low-fat or fat-free dairy products, such as milk, yogurt, or cheese?
- Do you eat 2 to 3 servings of lean meat, poultry, fish, dried beans, eggs, or nuts?
- Are you under sixty years of age?

If you're not answering yes, you may want to invest in a daily multivitamin and mineral supplement. These are not to be used in place of meals, of course, but to *supplement* them. One way to improve your eating habits in the meantime is to choose one food group at a time and strive to eat all of the servings for that group each day.

309. Make Sure Your Needs Are Being Met

People who may want to consider a multivitamin or mineral supplement to boost their metabolism include the following:

- Strict vegetarians may need extra calcium, iron, zinc, vitamin B12, and vitamin D.
- Women with heavy menstrual bleeding may need to replace iron each month.
- Women who are pregnant or breastfeeding (an activity beneficial to metabolism) need more of some nutrients. Be sure to speak with your doctor first.

- Menopausal women may need calcium supplements.
- People on a low-calorie diet can benefit from supplements.
- People over sixty years of age may have a decreased absorption of numerous vitamins and minerals.
- People who suffer from lactose intolerance or milk allergies may be advised to take a vitamin D and a calcium supplement.
- People with impaired nutrient absorption may be instructed by their doctor to take a supplement.
- People who regularly smoke and/or drink alcohol because these habits interfere with the body's ability to absorb and use certain vitamins and minerals will need supplements.

310. Familiarize Yourself with Vitamin Labeling Practices

Before learning why each vitamin is important and how much you need, it is crucial to understand how these values are generated. In the United States, the Food and Nutrition Board of the National Academy of Sciences / National Research Council is responsible for establishing and updating nutrition guidelines. The Recommended Dietary Allowances, or RDAs, have always been the benchmark for adequate nutritional intake in the United States. Based on scientific evidence, RDAs reflect the amount of a nutrient that is sufficient to meet the requirements of 97 to 98 percent of healthy individuals in a particular life stage and gender group.

311. Eat Biotin

The water-soluble nutrient known as biotin, or B7, biotin plays a key part in the formation of fatty acids and glucose (which are later broken down into energy) and in the metabolism of carbohydrates, fats, and proteins. It also helps to transfer carbon dioxide and generate energy during aerobic exercise when the body is engaged in the citric acid cycle. Though deficiency is rare, this nutrient can be found in healthy foods such as oatmeal, fortified cereals, Swiss chard, and eggs.

312. Consume Pantothenic Acid

This vitamin, also known as B5, is an extremely important piece of the metabolism pie. It metabolizes fats, carbohydrates, and proteins and is required to form an enzyme that breaks down fatty acids. By doing so, B5 helps your body produce energy. In addition, derivatives of pantothenic acid may improve the amount of fat contained in the blood and liver as well as lower LDL and triglyceride levels.

313. Try Sweet Potatoes

Sweet potatoes contain pantothenic acid. Try mashed sweet potatoes for a new take on an old favorite. Other sources include meat, poultry, fish, whole-grain cereals, legumes, yogurt, milk, and eggs.

314. Eat Vitamin A

If you munched on as many carrots as Bugs Bunny as a child and still ended up with glasses, don't think vitamin A let you down. You can blame genetics for that. Vitamin A, otherwise known as retinol, does promote the healthy development of cells and tissues—including those in your eyes—but it also strengthens the mucous membranes, which protect your body from invading viruses and bacteria, and it also stimulates bone growth. However, do keep in mind that while a serious deficiency of vitamin A can cause eye problems, dry skin, and reproductive problems, an excess of the nutrient can lead to nerve and liver damage, bone and joint pain, headaches, and in some cases, birth defects.

315. Try Winter Squash

One healthy way to make sure you have enough vitamin A in your diet is by eating winter squash; one serving contains about 145 percent of your dietary allowance. If you really want to make sure you've got enough though, munch on some raw carrots. They're tasty, low in calories, and have nearly 700 percent of the amount of beta-carotene you need for the day. If neither of those foods do it for you, try sweet potatoes, spinach, turnips, dark leafy greens, and apricots.

316. Meet Your Daily Beta

When ingested, the fat-soluble antioxidant beta-carotene is converted into vitamin A, which bolsters your ability to build healthy cells and tissues. Foods rich in beta-carotene include carrots, dark leafy greens, sweet potatoes, and mangos.

317. Dine on Vitamin D

You may know that vitamin D is a major player in developing strong bones and teeth and that it can be produced when the sun comes into contact with the skin. What you probably don't know is that endocrinologists recently linked weight loss success with the vitamin. Though the scientists still aren't sure why this was, the results of their study showed that for each milliliter increase in the hormonal form of the vitamin, the subjects lost nearly a quarter pound more, often in the abdominal area.

318. Try Mackerel

Mackerel and salmon are great sources of vitamin D because by eating just 3.5 ounces of either fish, you'll obtain 90 percent of your dietary allowance, plus some heart-healthy, metabolism-boosting omega-3s. Other healthy sources of vitamin D include milk, fortified cereal, and eggs.

319. Eat Vitamin E

By eating foods rich in vitamin E or by investing in a supplement that provides no more than 1,000 milligrams of the nutrient for adults—any more can cause adverse health effects—you can boost your memory and prevent damage caused by the breakdown of saturated fats—such as infertility and heart disease—especially if you take it along with the mineral selenium. So while you're boosting your metabolism, make sure to protect against those nasty free radicals and snap up some asparagus, beans, seeds, eggs, and healthy oils next time you're at the grocery store.

320. Try Peanut Butter

Peanut butter is not only a good source of protein and vitamin E, it is rich is magnesium, which is good for your metabolism. Other foods rich in vitamin E include dried almonds, vegetable oils, salad dressing, nuts and seeds, wheat germ oil, and green leafy vegetables.

321. Consume Vitamin K

This fat-soluble vitamin is important because of its ability to help create a protein that causes blood to clot, but it also helps to boost the metabolism by bonding calcium to bones (which increases bone mass). Less brittle bones reduce the likelihood of bone fractures during exercise or other activity. Though the vitamin is produced from the bacteria that live in your intestine, it can also be found in leafy greens, avocado, and kiwi. Ask your doctor before changing your vitamin K intake if you take the medication warfarin (Coumadin).

322. Try Turnip Greens

Turnip greens are good sources of vitamin K. Try them in a salad for a quick, healthy metabolism boost. Other foods rich in vitamin K include green leafy vegetables like spinach or kale, broccoli, cabbage, beef liver, egg yolk, and wheat bran or wheat germ.

323. Eat Folic Acid

Folic acid—a vitamin naturally found in leafy vegetables, oranges, wheat germ, and avocados—is critical to cell reproduction because it stabilizes DNA and, with the help of vitamin B12, aids in the production of hemoglobin. Metabolic benefits include regulating the body's insulin levels so it doesn't absorb unnecessary fat, and digesting and using proteins for energy with the help of B12 and vitamin C. For women who may become pregnant, researchers recommend a daily intake of 400 micrograms of folic acid per day from fortified foods or dietary supplements.

324. Consume Vitamin C (Ascorbic Acid)

Be honest, you probably don't take vitamin C until you have a cold—but you should. Its antioxidant properties lower the risk of heart disease by barring free radicals from building up on artery walls and causing atherosclerosis. It also improves blood pressure and, at levels of 1,000 to 2,000 milligrams, can help synthesize and thus reduce the effects of the amino acid homocysteine. On top of its heart-healthy benefits, vitamin C assists with the synthesizing of the amino acid carnitine, which in turn helps break down ingested fats. Beware of taking high doses of vitamin C supplements (more than 2,000 mg per day), however: This can cause nausea, diarrhea, kidney stones, and stomach inflammation.

325. Eat Mangos

Mangos are another excellent source of vitamin C. Try them in a smoothie for a refreshing midday snack. Other fruits and vegetables that are great sources of vitamin C include hot chili peppers (raw), cantaloupe, sweet peppers, dark green leafy vegetables, tomatoes, and oranges.

CHAPTER 21
Boost Your Metabolism by . . .
BEING B-VITAMIN SAVVY

Get Plenty of B Vitamins

Eat Thiamine (Vitamin B1)

Choose Foods Rich in Vitamin B1

Ingest Inositol

Consume Vitamin B2 (Riboflavin)

Choose Foods Rich in Vitamin B2

Try Niacin (Vitamin B3)

Don't Overdo Niacin

Load Up on Vitamin B6 (Pyridoxine)

Don't Overdo B6

Fill Up with Folate

Eat Vitamin B12 (Cyanocobalamin)

Consume Pantothenic Acid (Vitamin B5)

Get Plenty of Coenzyme Q10

326. Get Plenty of B Vitamins

B vitamins have the power to boost your energy, and thus your metabolism. They are particularly important for helping your body process fats, carbohydrates, and protein into energy. Consider them combustion fuel and make sure to eat a diet rich in B vitamins and to supplement your diet with extra B, especially when you are under a great deal of stress. Wherever possible, choose foods high in B vitamins, and add supplements if you aren't getting enough B vitamins or if you need a boost to jump-start metabolism. B12 in particular can help improve flagging energy.

327. Eat Thiamine (Vitamin B1)

Thiamine is needed to help produce energy from the carbohydrates that you eat. It also is required for normal functioning of all body cells, especially nerves. A thiamine deficiency can lead to beriberi (an ailment of the nervous system), fatigue, mental confusion, loss of energy, nerve damage, muscle weakness, and impaired growth. This condition is very rare in the United States because most people consume plenty of grain products. Since thiamine is a water-soluble vitamin, the body excretes excess amounts that you consume, so nothing is left behind to slow down your metabolism or increase your weight.

328. Choose Foods Rich in Vitamin B1

Foods rich in thiamine include whole-grain foods, enriched-grain foods, fortified cereals, beef liver, pork, and wheat germ.

329. Ingest Inositol

Not only does a high-fiber diet cause your body to burn more energy during the digestive process, it also is the best way to make sure you get enough inositol. The nutrient, once known as B8, is crucial for the muscular and nervous systems to work effectively, and may improve the mood of those suffering from depression. Along with folacin, vitamins B6 and B12, choline, betaine, and methionine, inositol stops fat from building up in the liver, and it helps in the digestion of fat and reducing blood cholesterol levels.

330. Consume Vitamin B2 (Riboflavin)

Just like thiamine, riboflavin plays a key role in releasing energy from the macronutrients to all cells of the body. Riboflavin also helps change the amino acid (building blocks of protein) tryptophan into niacin, another B vitamin. Riboflavin is important in normal growth, production of certain hormones, formation of red blood cells, and in vision and skin health. A deficiency of riboflavin is unlikely but can cause eye disorders, dry and flaky skin, and burning and dryness of the mouth and tongue. There are no reported problems from overconsumption, but moderation is the best policy.

331. Choose Foods Rich in Vitamin B2

Foods rich in riboflavin (vitamin B2) include beef liver, milk, low-fat yogurt, cheese, enriched-grain foods, whole-grain foods, eggs, and green leafy vegetables.

332. Try Niacin (Vitamin B3)

More commonly known as niacin, vitamin B3 is instrumental in maintaining the health of the skin, nerves, and digestive system. It also helps release energy from food, aids in the synthesis of DNA, and helps lower blood levels of cholesterol and triglycerides.

333. Don't Overdo Niacin

In large doses, niacin has been used as a cholesterol-lowering supplement. Because large doses can cause symptoms such as flushed skin, rashes, and even liver damage, this should only be done under a doctor's supervision. Protect your body by gaining most of niacin from food sources, such as whole-grain foods, fortified cereal, lean meats, fish, poultry, peanuts, brewer's yeast, yogurt, and sunflower seeds.

334. Load Up on Vitamin B6 (Pyridoxine)

This helpful vitamin is found in three forms (pyridoxine in plant foods, pyridoxal and pyridoxamine in animal foods), but the one we ingest most often is pyridoxine. It is a key element used in the metabolic breakdown of certain fats found in plants and animals. When it comes to turning your body into a fat-burning machine, pyridoxine assists by improving the body's reaction to stress and supplying muscles with much-needed energy.

335. Don't Overdo B6

Don't exceed 100 milligrams a day without checking with your doctor; excess can be toxic. Instead of relying on vitamin supplements, load your diet with foods rich in the vitamin: liver, beef, chicken, fish, bananas, carrots, lentils, rice, soybeans, whole grains, and avocados.

336. Fill Up with Folate

Folate (another B vitamin), taken in conjunction with vitamin B6, fosters the health of red blood cells, and healthy red blood cells are needed to transport oxygen to muscles, fueling the metabolic fires. Great sources for folate are dark leafy greens, romaine lettuce, asparagus, broccoli, cauliflower, beets, and lentils.

337. Eat Vitamin B12 (Cyanocobalamin)

Supplement your diet with B12 and you may find that your mood improves, you sleep better, and you have a newfound knack for remembering where you put your car keys. If you take it with B6 and folate, cyanocobalamin can help lower levels of homocysteine, an amino acid that can cause arterial breakdown. It helps boost metabolism by aiding digestion and nutrient absorption, so remember to add it to your diet by dining on enriched dairy products, beef, poultry, tuna and certain shellfish, beef, oysters, crab, and tuna. Vegetarians may need supplemental vitamins.

338. Consume Pantothenic Acid (Vitamin B5)

Pantothenic acid is utilized in the formation of coenzymes, which are equally important in about a hundred metabolic reactions. These processes include energy production, fatty acid catabolism, fatty acid synthesis, and cholesterol, phospholipid, and steroid hormone production, among many others. This vitamin helps the body absorb and properly use other vitamins in the body, such as 6, B12, and C. It also helps produce vitamin D. In addition, vitamin B5 is important to maintain a healthy digestive tract and to break down carbohydrates, fats, lipids, and various amino acids. Pantothenic acid can be found in corn, eggs, cheese, meat, peanuts, liver, soy products, peas, broccoli, tomatoes, and whole grains.

339. Get Plenty of Coenzyme Q10

Aging leads to a decline in energy metabolism in many tissues, especially liver, heart, and skeletal muscle. Decreasing levels of coenzyme Q10, a vitamin-like substance, as we age may play a role in this decline. Coenzyme Q10 or CoQ10 is used to treat several disorders related to suboptimal cellular energy metabolism and oxidative injury and has also been shown to be useful in alleviating the effects of abnormalities involving the heart's ability to contract and pump blood effectively, such as congestive heart failure and a number of heart muscle diseases. CoQ10 also appears to work with vitamin E to help prevent the oxidation of low-density lipoprotein (LDL, or "bad" cholesterol). It's believed that oxidized LDL can lead to plaque buildup, clogged arteries, and an increased risk of heart attack or stroke. CoQ10 may reduce the ability of blood to clot, thereby decreasing the chance of a blood clot getting stuck in a clogged artery and causing a heart attack or stroke. Other heart-related conditions for which CoQ10 supplementation shows promise include hypertension and heart valve replacement. To bulk up on CoQ10 eat sardines, mackerel, nuts, organ meats, beef, broccoli, chicken, oranges, salmon, or trout.

If you have heart disease you should talk to your doctor before taking CoQ10. Organ damage due to the lack of oxygen / blood flow during intense exercise has been reported in a study of patients with this disease, although the specific role of CoQ10 is not clear. Vigorous exercise is often discouraged in people using CoQ10 supplements.

CHAPTER 22

Boost Your Metabolism by . . .

TRYING SUPPLEMENTS

Arm Yourself with Knowledge

Take Fish Oil Capsules

Try Pancreatin

Try Alpha Lipoic Acid

Try Proteolytic Enzymes

Try Vanadium

Try Schizandra

Try Resveratrol

Try Ginseng

Try Carnitine

340. Arm Yourself with Knowledge

Throughout this book, we have stressed that the first and best things you can do to improve your metabolism are to improve your overall health, nourish your body with ideal proportions of a variety of healthy food choices, and lead an active life that includes regular aerobic exercise. Once you have taken these steps, you may want to explore other supplements that can provide additional nutrients to your body as well as short-term and long-term health and metabolism benefits with very little effort. However, David Grotto, RD, a spokesperson for the American Dietetic Association, warns, "Supplements can enhance a diet where there are shortfalls, but a handful of vitamin, mineral, or other dietary supplements can never take the place of a healthy diet."

Please note that just because a supplement is labeled *natural* or *herbal* does not mean that it's inherently safe. Be sure to consult your physician before starting, or radically changing, any physical, nutritional, or supplemental regimen. Some supplements may interact with other medications or other supplements, and some may be dangerous if you take too many.

341. Take Fish Oil Capsules

Over the years, fish oil has been touted to help with a myriad of medical problems—including protecting the body from the onset of Parkinson's and schizophrenia—but what is very exciting is its ability (because of the high levels of omega-3 it contains) to lower the body's cholesterol levels, reduce overall blood pressure, and keep you full for longer. There is also recent evidence from the *International Journal of Obesity* that suggests fish oil helps with the body's ability to burn fat and that those who supplement with fish oil will metabolize more fat as they exercise. When you're looking for a fish oil supplement, reach for those containing 300 milligrams of the fatty acid EPA and 200 milligrams of the fatty acid DHA and take two each day. Ask your doctor before taking omega-3 supplements if you have an increased risk of bleeding.

342. Try Pancreatin

Pancreatin, or pancreatic acid, is a combination of the pancreatic enzymes lipase, protease, and amylase, which improves digestion by signaling more digestive enzymes to take on the task. These enzymes help the body to be more effective at breaking down fats, starches, and complex proteins into nutrients so they can be absorbed into the body.

Be sure to take only the recommended dose of this supplement as high doses can cause problems such as colon damage and high blood levels of a dangerous substance called uric acid.

343. Try Alpha Lipoic Acid

Alpha lipoic acid is a fatty acid found in each cell in the human body and in limited amounts in foods rich in lipoyllysine. These foods include spinach, broccoli, and organ meats. As an antioxidant that is both water and fat soluble, it can protect against free radicals throughout the body, including those created during the synthesis of vitamin E. However, its primary function is to covert glucose into energy, which boosts metabolism.

344. Try Proteolytic Enzymes

Proteolytic enzymes help regulate protein function. Your body produces these enzymes naturally, but production slows as you age. Some of the food you eat—cooked or processed meat, for example—causes the enzymes to be diverted from their main role to help digest the food. Proteolytic enzymes also combat inflammation by neutralizing biochemicals associated with the problem. Between the body's natural slowdown in enzyme production and diversion of the enzymes for digestion, you are losing a soldier, so to speak, in the battle against inflammation caused by free radical damage. Supplements work well in replacing those lost enzymes. You can find proteolytic enzyme supplements at any health food store.

345. Try Vanadium

Mushrooms, black pepper, parsley, dill weed, and whole grains contain vanadium, a compound that boosts your body's sensitivity to insulin, which you need to properly process calories and thereby stabilize your blood sugar. You can also take supplements containing vanadium, but it can be toxic. DO NOT EXCEED 1.8 milligrams daily. People with kidney disease should not take vanadium and the recommended doses should be adhered to as high doses of vanadium (more than 1.8 mg per day) may cause liver or kidney damage.

346. Try Schizandra

Schizandra berries, also known as the "five flavor fruit" because they stimulate all five of the taste buds, have been used in Chinese medicine for centuries. The herb reduces the body's response to stressful situations, but herbalists believe that it can also improve endurance, mental alertness, and aid metabolism by regulating blood sugar levels. In addition, it is said to help detoxify the liver and improve the workings of many of the body's organ systems.

347. Try Resveratrol

It appears that resveratrol, an antioxidant found in red wine, is the key to unlocking the maddening "French Paradox." Though, at this juncture, most of the research has been conducted on nonhuman species, those studies suggest that the fat-soluble compound helps the liver to process carbohydrates—boosting metabolism. Resveratrol acts as an antioxidant and may help to protect against atherosclerosis and heart disease. It also activates SIRT1, a gene that helps the body process fat, improves overall aerobic activity, and may have a positive impact on longevity. Resveratrol should not be used with drugs that increase risk of bleeding, including warfarin/Coumadin, aspirin, heparin, and lovenox. Until more is known about the estrogenic activity of resveratrol in humans, women with a history of estrogen-sensitive cancers, such as breast, ovarian, and uterine cancers, should avoid resveratrol supplements.

348. Try Ginseng

Ginseng has many beneficial effects. It has been used for thousands of years by herbalists to reduce cholesterol levels, increase the absorption of nutrients through the intestinal walls, mop up free radicals in the blood, and protect against cancer. Ginseng may decrease muscle injury and inflammation following exercise, and some studies suggest that it may reduce oxidation of LDL ("bad") cholesterol and brain tissue. This herb can also boost your metabolism. It does so primarily by alleviating stress and by reducing the amount of carbohydrates that are processed into your bloodstream and cause your glucose levels to spike. People scheduled for surgeries should stop taking ginseng a week before surgery and caution should also be practiced if taking anticoagulants. Patients with hormone-sensitive diseases—like certain cancers—should not consume ginseng.

349. Try Carnitine

Carnitine is a naturally occurring amino-acid derivative that helps the body convert fat into energy. After you eat, the compound takes the fatty acid molecules from your food and brings them into a cell's mitochondria so they can be broken down and used for energy. Though carnitine is usually found in the skeletal muscles, heart, brain, and sperm in adequate quantities, you can turn to red meat and dairy for an extra boost.

People with certain conditions such as peripheral vascular disease, hypertension (high blood pressure), alcohol-induced liver disease (cirrhosis), diabetes, and kidney disease should talk to their doctor before taking carnitine. Also talk to your doctor if you are taking AZT, doxorubicin, isotretinoin, or valproic acid.

CHAPTER 23

Boost Your Metabolism by . . .

REDUCING STRESS

De-Stress Yourself

Think Holistically

Try Yoga

Embrace Pilates

Get a Massage

Try Acupuncture

Laugh

Meditate

Try Aromatherapy

Practice Time Management

Get Plenty of Sleep

Sit in the Sunshine

Pursue a Hobby

Listen to Relaxing Music

Practice Deep Breathing

Plant and Maintain a Vegetable or Herb Garden

350. De-Stress Yourself

By this point, we know that our emotional, mental, and physical selves are intertwined and interlinked. We have ample evidence to prove that our psychological health affects our physical health, and vice versa. To this end, you need to realize that stress—especially long-term stress—has a negative effect on your body and your metabolism. A body that is under stress produces cortisol, a hormone left over from the days when our fight or flight response was necessary for survival. Back in the day, cortisol left the body after the appropriate response was taken, but long-term stress causes the hormone to take up residence in your body. This disruption to your system causes weight gain, depression, and a decreased metabolism. To de-stress your body—and boost your metabolism—take the following steps. You'll be glad you did!

351. Think Holistically

It's vital to your overall health to think holistically—to view yourself as a whole being, not a collection of parts. In the 1970s, when Buddhist ideas seeped into Western culture, one essential message was: "I am not my liver, my spleen, my blood, nor my brain. I am all of me." It sounded new and often revolutionary at the time, but science soon joined the chorus. You are not the sum of all your parts; you are the sum of all your parts operating in tandem. Mind, body, and spirit are inseparable, and illness in one often produces illness in the others. Think holistically, and your overall health, as well as your rate of metabolism, will improve. Check out these alternative practices: tai chi, qigong, or Reiki.

352. Try Yoga

Yoga is a great way to build additional strength and flexibility without pounding your muscles as aerobic exercises tend to do. Stretching brings everything back into balance, keeping your muscles soft and supple so they can do their job. Since muscles help maintain posture and balance, helping them maintain pliability and strength will boost your overall health and your muscles' ability to burn fat.

353. Embrace Pilates

Pilates is a series of exercises that focus on strengthening core postural muscles to support the spine for correct alignment, an approach used by many hospital rehabilitation programs. Recently, Pilates has become very popular with the general public, particularly those who are looking for a gentle method of increasing core strength, flexibility, and movement.

Pilates is typically taught in health clubs, where private or semiprivate instruction is available on special equipment or group mat classes are conducted without equipment. Pilates uses the resistance of the body to condition and correct itself, with the goal of lengthening and aligning the spine. Like yoga, Pilates offers a low-impact form of strengthening and toning muscles while helping you get more in tune with your body.

The practice focuses on the deep and lateral transverse abdominal muscle, combining stretching and strengthening exercises that target the abdominals, gluteals, and lower-back muscles. It can benefit athletes, those recovering from injuries, and everyone in between.

354. Get a Massage

High stress levels can contribute to your body storing extra fat, so it's important to incorporate relaxation moments into your weeks. One great way to do this is through regular massages. Not only do they feel great, they also improve muscle flexibility and have been shown to improve circulation, which helps to boost metabolism.

355. Try Acupuncture

Many people have found acupuncture effective in maintaining a healthy weight and increasing their metabolism. Acupuncture treatments are typically achieved by the placement of slender needles in areas of the person's body that have to do with appetite control, sugar imbalances, water retention, impulsive eating, thyroid stimulation, and weight gain associated with menopause or premenstrual syndrome.

356. Laugh

Not only does laughing ratchet down your stress level instantaneously, a study by Vanderbilt University reported a 20 percent boost in metabolism after laughing. Even if you're not feeling particularly joyful, try forcing a laugh anyway. There's a good chance that just trying to laugh will lift your mood and metabolism.

357. Meditate

Take up meditation and other stress-reducing techniques. Fifteen minutes of uninterrupted meditation is a wonderful way to melt away the day's worries and stress. Meditation has also been said to increase energy levels and stimulate metabolism.

358. Try Aromatherapy

Many essential oils, such as lavender, have proven stress-reducing qualities. A warm, lavender-scented bath, for example, is a great way to relax and unwind. It also promotes restful sleep.

359. Practice Time Management

Improve your time management at work and at home so that you're not constantly playing catch-up. This will reduce your stress level and help you stay committed to a healthy eating plan and lifestyle. Always schedule time for relaxation and exercise.

360. Get Plenty of Sleep

Your body actually mends and maintains itself when you sleep. If you strength-train or do any sort of resistance exercise, then your muscles repair themselves and grow stronger when you're asleep. If you don't sleep, your muscles will stay fatigued and not get stronger. When you sleep less than you should, your body loses leptin and ghrelin, two hormones that help regulate energy use and appetite. Researchers at Stanford University found that people who snoozed fewer than 7.5 hours per night experienced an increase in their body mass index. To maintain strong muscles, you need at least 8 hours of sleep. It's helpful to first recognize that you want to sleep well (i.e., 7 to 9 hours of uninterrupted sleep each night). Go to sleep and wake up at the same times. Your body loves regularity.

361. Sit in the Sunshine

Not only does it feel good, but sitting in sunlight decreases melatonin and increases serotonin, which helps your body feel fully awake and your metabolic rate increase. The sun's rays also provide a major source of vitamin D—a metabolism booster. If you are locked up inside all day, find 10 minutes in your day to go out into the sunshine and soak up some rays.

362. Pursue a Hobby

A calming activity such as gardening or painting is a great way to forget your troubles and relax. Choose something that energizes your spirit while relaxing your mind.

363. Listen to Relaxing Music

Listening to music that has a calming effect has been shown to reduce cortisol, one of the primary hormones that negatively affect metabolism. And when you're ready to rock again, switch to music that leaves you feeling energized; it will raise your heart and breathing rates, boosting metabolism.

364. Practice Deep Breathing

Breathing keeps you alive; breathing deeply keeps blood and oxygen coursing through your veins, which is crucial to effective metabolism. Don't just breathe; inhale deeply, slowly drawing breaths into your abdomen and slowly exhaling. As you are breathing, imagine the blood being pushed out of your internal organs as you breathe in and then oxygenated blood rushing back in as you exhale.

365. Plant and Maintain a Vegetable or Herb Garden

Gardening not only gives you the opportunity to work out in the fresh air, it burns calories and helps you make healthier food choices on a daily basis. Plus, nothing beats fresh-picked vegetables and herbs when you want to eat healthfully and intensify the taste of salsas, sauces, and savory dishes. Tending to your garden, particularly using a spade to turn over dirt and dig in fertilizers and soil amendments, provides a regular workout that increases your metabolism through exercise. Plus, if you love to cook and also appreciate having fresh vegetables and herbs packed with vitamins, minerals, and other nutrients, having your own vegetable and herb garden will encourage you to eat healthier—every day.

INDEX

About the Author

Rachel Laferriere, MS, RD, received her BS in Dietetics from the University of Rhode Island and her MS in Clinical Nutrition from Tufts University's Friedman School of Nutrition Science and Policy. She completed her dietetic internship at the Frances Stern Nutrition Center at Tufts Medical Center. Ms. Laferriere is a Licensed Dietitian/Nutritionist in Rhode Island and a Certified Nutrition Support Dietitian. She currently works with adult patients as a clinical dietitian. Her work has been published in the *Tufts Daily* newspaper and *Nutrition in Clinical Care*.